D0569791

PAGAN CHRISTS

PAGAN CHRISTS

By J. M. Robertson

DORSET PRESS
New York

This edition published by Dorset Press,
a division of
Marboro Books Corporation,
by arrangement with
Lyle Stuart, Inc.
1987 Dorset Press

ISBN 0-88029-1441-9

Printed in the United States of America

M 9 8 7 6 5 4 3 2

Contents

Introduction

The first edition of *Pagan Christs* was published in 1903 and was intended to complete the task J. M. Robertson began in an earlier volume, *Christianity and Mythology*. His main aim was to show that alleged historical events on which Christianity was based had never occurred, and that the reputed Founder of Christianity had never existed. The myth theory goes back to the eighteenth century when Volney argued that Jesus was a solar myth derived from Krishna. In 1840 Bruno Bauer contended that Jesus was an invention of Mark. In the first decade of the present century there was widespread interest in the myth theory and the works of Thomas Whittaker, W. B. Smith and Arthur Drews—variants which differed from Robertson in detail. They relied on the wealth of data on anthropology and comparative religion which was contained in the massive studies of Frazer, Jevons, Durkheim and others, as well as the new light thrown on biblical origins. Robertson's most distinctive thesis is that the Gospel story of the Last Supper, the Agony, the Betrayal, the Crucifixion and the Resurrection was a mystery play which came to be accepted as an account of real happenings. The origin of this ritual drama is an ancient Palestinian rite in which an annual victim, known as "Jesus (Joshua) the Son of the Father" was actually sacrificed.

Passion plays were a common feature of the popular religion of Greece and Egypt. Like Christ, such pagan gods as Adonis, Attis, Osiris and Dionysus were slain in periodical mimicry, only to rise again in triumph. Robertson's thesis is that the make-believe of drama is an evolution from the more primitive and savage reality of human sacrifice. In *Pagan Christs* he therefore assembles an impressive body of evidence showing how the evolution of religious ideas and practices follows a similar pattern throughout the world. As civilization progresses the sacrifice of the son of the ancient king was modified by the use of a surrogate—either a criminal or an animal. The collective eating of the victim—cannibalism in its earliest phase—gave rise to symbolic communion with bread and wine. Parallel rites to the Christian eucharist are found in the worship of Mithra and Dionysus and the gods of ancient Mexico.

Another line of evolution is from the primary god to the secondary or Teaching god. In most ancient religions there are myths of divine Teachers who were lawgivers or who introduced agriculture, writing and building. These secondary gods may or may not be both sacrificed saviors and teachers. Jesus Christ was both. Buddha was not sacrificed, but he satisfied the craving for a Teacher who would provide moral instruction and the way of salvation. But Gotama was as mythical as Mithra and Christ.

The vast canvas employed by Robertson was necessary when he advanced his theory for the consideration of contemporary scholars; but for the nonspecialist reader the complexity of the argument and the abundance of detail undoubtedly distract attention from the essential outline of the mythicist case. In this edition the original version has been pruned to enable the ordinary reader to see the wood that may have seemed obscured by the trees. Lengthy refutations of now forgotten authors and references to books that are either obsolete or inaccessible have been eliminated. Inevitably this has involved some simplification of the presentation. Robertson's mind was so loaded with obscure knowledge that the sheer weight of erudition is sometimes in danger of defeating its object except for those whose scholarship is as profound—and they are few.

The fact that since Robertson's death the mythicist case has been regarded as unfashionable may not be unconnected with the virtual disappearance of biblical scholars who are not clergymen. The discovery of the Dead Sea Scrolls may well lend new and powerful arguments in its favor. No one would have been more delighted than Robertson by the sort of developments hinted at by Mr. John Allegro. But *Pagan Christs* can bear the most critical scrutiny and stand on its own merits. The information it contains about the brutal and bizarre world of religious fantasy is as astonishing as it is sobering.

* * * * *

John Mackinnon Robertson was born in the Isle of Arran on November 14, 1856 and died in 1933. He left school at the age of thirteen and after that was entirely self-educated. Despite early handicaps his indomitable will and energy enabled him to master completely six languages and acquire the erudition which qualified him to compete on equal terms with leading scholars of the day. Not only was he recognized as an authority on comparative religion—which he preferred to call 'hierology' —but he was also a Shakespearean scholar of distinction. As a young man he entered newspaper journalism which seemed in his circumstances to hold the most promising opportunities. He was a leader writer on the staff of the *Edinburg Evening News* until 1884 when he was invited by Charles Bradlaugh to come to London and contribute regularly to the *National Reformer.* When Bradlaugh died he became editor of this freethought journal, and when it ceased publication owing to financial difficulties he launched the *Free Review.* This was transformed four years later into the *University Magazine and Free Review.*

In 1897–8 Robertson lectured throughout the United States and in 1900 he accepted a commission from the *Morning Leader* to visit South Africa and report on the working of martial law. His literary output in articles and books was enormous and yet he found time to play a prominent part in the political arena. He was elected Member of Parliament for Tyneside in the great Liberal landslide of 1906. During his thirteen years in Parliament he surprised many who had looked upon him as a scholar absorbed in mainly academic interests. He made his mark in the debates on Free Trade and showed himself to be a capable administrator and man of affairs. He was Parliamentary Secretary to the Board of Trade from 1911 to 1915, when he was made a Privy Councillor.

There can be no doubt that of all the fields his powerful intellect explored religious controversy was nearest his heart. He was one of the leading exponents of what came to be known as the 'mythicist' theory of Christianity. This is developed in *Christianity and Mythology*, which was followed by *Pagan Christs*

(1903). Of his historical studies the *History of Freethought in the Nineteenth Century* and *A Short History of Freethought* are still the most authoritative works on the subject. He wrote prolifically on politics, sociology, and literary criticism, and among these books may be mentioned *Modern Humanists*, *An Introduction to English Politics*, *Montaigne and Shakespeare* and *Did Shakespeare write Titus Andronicus*?

Although not an orator gifted with the eloquence of Bradlaugh and Ingersoll, Robertson was a highly effective platform speaker. He did not suffer fools gladly and his polemics were characterized by an asperity and sometimes harshness. Meticulously careful in verifying facts he was merciless in his exposure of slipshod argument and woolly thinking.

The main theme of this book is that religion, as we know it today, has evolved from primitive concepts and savage rites, including human sacrifice and cannibalism. So far from Christianity being an exception it is a conspicuous example of such a development. The history of religion is a history of the manufacture of gods by men. The primary objects of worship give ground in course of time to secondary gods. Most of these are lawgivers and moral teachers; some are saviors who are sacrificed and brought to life again. The various savior-gods, whose death and resurrection are periodically celebrated, give this book its title of *Pagan Christs*.

Whereas it is generally supposed that Jesus Christ was a real person who was crucified in Palestine by order of Pontius Pilate, no one seriously claims that Adonis, Attis and Osiris were historical characters. Similarly, Mithra, whose cult rivalled Christianity throughout the Roman Empire, and Huitzilopochtli and Quetzalcoatl, the gods of ancient Mexico, seem obviously mythical. Why, then, is an exception made of the alleged Founder of Christianity? It cannot be because the miraculous events associated with the 'Pagan Christs' are incredible; they are no more so than the Gospel narratives. The fact that the religions of ancient Egypt, Greece and Mexico have no followers today does not disprove their claims. A story may be true even though nobody believes it. Finally, it may be contended that Christianity introduced a new ethical message, therefore it must have been the creation of a remarkable personality. Such a tremendous innovation cannot have arisen spontaneously. Like Buddhism and Mohammedanism, the teaching bears the stamp of religious genius at the very least.

In order to deal with these objections and establish a case in favor of the theory that Jesus is as mythical as Attis and Osiris, it is necessary to show that all the savior-gods, throughout the world, have common features due to common antecedents. It is not that all these cults need have originated in one centre from which they were dispersed, but that they have all evolved from the same type of primitive ritual, namely human sacrifice. We know that in Mexico and Peru human sacrifice on a huge scale was practised in the sixteenth century A.D. In the Graeco-Roman world, however, it had virtually died out at the beginning of our era. That it was once prevalent in the Middle East, including Palestine, is quite certain, and the story of Abraham and Isaac is one of the pointers to the practice of human sacrifice by the earliest Hebrews.

The general pattern of sacrificial rituals down to the time of Christianity can be traced as follows:

All victims, animal or human, were slain and then eaten. Apart from offerings to the gods there were two types of sacrifice: (1) Totem-sacrifices, in which the victim was either eaten as the god or as a mode of union with the divine ancestor or as a totem species; (2) Human sacrifices, usually involving prisoners of war, who were eaten for a variety of reasons. They could be thank-offerings for victory, they might be 'sin' offerings, or vegetation charms, or serve the purpose of sanctifying new buildings.

At a later stage we find the idea of priestly efficacy in which the sacramental meal is blessed by a sacerdotal caste. When this requires human sacrifice the victim (a) represents the god, (b) is a king or a king's son, (c) is a first-born or only son. From this barbarous beginning the use of surrogates is a natural step towards more civilized societies. Animals then take the place of the human victim, and when even animal sacrifices become objectionable the ancient rite is performed symbolically. There is a mystery drama, for example, in which an actor impersonates an unjustly slain god. With the further growth of a priesthood an official ritual is fashioned and what was once a cannibal feast is refined into a symbolical communion, bread and wine being substituted for real flesh and blood.

Christianity is not unique in this respect. Eucharistic rituals are prefigured in the Zoroastrian deification of a special liquid (Haoma) and in the Vedic drink, Soma, of India. In the worship of Dionysos communion with the god is by means of wine. In the Mithra rite communion is effected by bread and water, and the early Christians were so shocked by its resemblance to their own Lord's Supper that they described it as an invention of the devil to deceive the faithful. There were other, striking parallels even more plainly related to a savage past. Salvation and eternal life were conferred on the Mithraist by being baptised either with the blood of a bull or that of a ram, hence the derivation of the phrase 'washed in the blood of the lamb,' and the invocation 'Agnus dei qui tollis peccata mundi' (Lamb of God that taketh away the sin of the world).

The close connection of the central rite of the Christian Church with similar rites which are themselves refinements of a primeval custom of human sacrifice does not dispose of the historicity of Christ though it raises considerable doubt. It calls for a re-examination of the Gospel story in the light of what is known of ancient religion. For if in the pre-Christian era ritual sacrifice sometimes gave place to a Passion play, is it not possible that the Gospel narrative may not be history but the script of a drama? Such an hypothesis can be tested in several ways. It would receive confirmation if some of the details can be shown to be parallel to the procedures of primitive human sacrifice; and further, if the stage limitations of time and space would explain some puzzling inconsistencies in the story.

There are many examples in early religions of the human victim of ritual sacrifice being deified in the process. An instance which fortunately came under the notice of a scientific observer occurred as late as the middle of the nineteenth century in the Indian province of Orissa. The Khonds, an aboriginal hill tribe, have a supply of victims who know they will be sacrificed one day. They have either been bought as children, or they have volunteered, since by such a death they are made gods. They are slain while bound to a cross, but at one stage they are given a stupefying drug and their legs are broken.

The most significant parallels in the Khond rite and the Christian crucifixion are the cross, the merciful offer of a drink, the fact that the god-man victim is willing and yet 'bought with a price.' Normally the legs of Christ would have been broken, as this was common practice in many forms of animal and human sacrifice. At a higher stage of evolution, however, it is felt that a maimed victim is unseemly.

Among the Semites there is a tradition that the sacrifice by a king of his son is extremely efficacious. The reference in Matthew 27.16.17 to Barrabas was long accepted in the primitive church to read 'Jesus Barrabas,' and this is translated 'Son of the Father.' There are grounds for surmising a pre-Christian cult of Jesus (Joshua), associated in remote times with human sacrifice. Other influences were also at work in fashioning the Christian mystery drama, notably the widespread myths of a dying and resurrected god and the sacrifice of a mock-king at Rhodes at the feats of Kronos. In Semitic mythology Kronos 'whom the Phoenicians call Israel' sacrifices his only son after putting upon him royal robes. In the historical period the victim who played the part of the king's son was a condemned criminal.

The mock-crowning and robing of Christ recalls, too, the Sacaea ceremony of ancient Babylon. In all cases where an annual victim may have been hard to procure there was the bait of unlimited luxury and license for a year. At the end of this period, in Asia as in Mexico, the victim had to be discredited before being slain. It was also common practice to offer a narcotic to deaden pain during the execution.

Throughout Egypt and the Middle East it is an unquestionable fact that mystery plays were performed which enacted a ritual sacrifice. The Egyptians played the death of Osiris. Effigies of Adonis and Attis were used in representations of their death and resurrection. So, too, Mithra's burial and triumphant rising from the tomb. It would not be surprising if the Christian story were also dramatised. Paul, in Galatians (iii-I) seems to refer to the impersonation of Christ crucified. One proof that the story of the Supper, Passion, Betrayal, Trial and Crucifixion is based on a drama is given in the compression of the events for obviously theatrical reasons. One striking piece of evidence is the prayer put into the mouth of Jesus when no one could have heard what he said. Only in transcription from a dramatic text could such incongruities have arisen.

One of the objections brought against the myth theory is that such a lofty ethical teaching as is contained in the New Testament could only have originated in a religious genius. Against this argument it can be shown that the ethical content of the Gospels contains nothing that is not found in the Old Testament. And of all religions the one that lays most emphasis on ethics—at least in its pristine form—is Buddhism. Yet the teaching of Gotama was not committed to writing for long after his presumed death, and there were many other 'Buddhas,' since 'Buddha' like 'Christ' is a title, not a proper name.

In the history of religion there are many Teaching gods, but few would be claimed as real by the secular historian. Mohammed is an exception. He founded a new religion and there is sound evidence of the circumstances of his life, but he has never been deified. Although Gotama is not a god he is regarded as a superhuman being and his biography contains the usual cluster of legend. He belongs to myth, not history.

The 'Christs' of the world function as secondary, Teaching gods, whatever theological or metaphysical explanations are provided by their followers. Paradoxically enough, the highest ethical teaching is sometimes combined with savage and bloodthirsty rites. In ancient Mexico the priesthood were mostly celibate, and they taught the people to be peaceful, to bear injuries with meekness and to be compassionate to the sick and the poor. Yet they indulged in mass human sacrifices.

In the case of Mithraism and Christianity the memory of this primitive and barbaric cult was lost, but the vestigial remains can be recognized under the symbolic guise of religious drama. What was once the literal eating of a supposedly divine victim became communion with the god in a symbolic rite. Those who devoutly participated in the dramatic representation of death and resurrection and in eating the god became convinced that Mithra or Christ were real persons. Like many other savior gods, they were personifications that emerged from a rite, and their doctrines reflected human aspiration.

London
May 1966 — Hector Hawton

PAGAN CHRISTS

Chapter One

RELIGION IN THE MAKING

Petronius was surely right in saying *Fear made the gods*. In primitive times fear of *the* unknown was normal; gratitude to *an* unknown was impossible. Other motives came into play at a later stage, but even so the feeling of gratitude to God in the higher religions was often related to fear of the evil spirits whom he wards off. There is nothing particularly ethical in thanking Providence for saving one from an earthquake in which many other people have perished.

We cannot make a sharp distinction between the Gods of fear and the Gods of love. Nevertheless, certain deities are so largely shaped by men's affections that they might be termed the Beloved Gods. They could be called the *Christs* of the world's pantheon. Such a title would include some figures which do not strictly rank as Gods, but if we approach religious history in this way we shall see that the religions of mankind are all man-made. This does not commit us at the outset to an opinion, for example, about the historicity of a Christ or a Buddha. The point is that all primitive beliefs and practices, however strange and absurd, can be understood as natural products. They are derived from mistaken judgments about causation and the nature of things.

For primitive man there were no conceptual divisions between religion and science, worship and art. Magic and taboo do not belong to an earlier stage which was then superseded by religion. Religion itself is permeated by magic. Thus the primitive sacramental meal was clearly based on sympathetic magic. It was a way of making friends with the God by fraternizing with men.

The theory that religion is not only hostile to magic but quite separate from it is as fallacious as the distinction between religion and superstition. As Hobbes pointed out, religion is "what is allowed," superstition what is "not allowed." Again, it is not true to say that "religious" magic aims at public good and "mere" magic at private harm. The public magician is often notoriously a murdering scoundrel, whereas the private sorcerer may be an innocent man done to death.

If magic and religion were quite separate Elijah would have to be regarded as an irreligious magician. According to the legend, he called down fire from heaven and therefore acted like a sorcerer with absolute confidence in his power to control the will of God. It will not do to say that this was a demonstration of faith rather than magic if at the same time we condemn the faith of the ordinary magician to control the Gods.

When we seriously inquire which has done more harm in hindering progress, strangling science and prompting human cruelty, I think it will soon be found that the organized cults which condemn the magician have been far more pernicious. The evil done by the superstitious few who practiced witchcraft was trifling compared with the no less superstitious many who put the witches to death. The priests of the Christian Church have always been hostile to magic while assuming magical functions themselves. The eucharist, which developed into a State cult in Europe, is really a form of sympathetic magic. So, too, the claim of priests to use such supernatural instruments as holy relics, and to possess the powers of exorcism, shows how deeply magic is embedded in religion.

Magic and religion are interconnected because both evolved from an animistic view of nature. Early man conceived of nature in terms of his own moral ideas. It was therefore inevitable that he should alternately resort to propitiation and magic, and feel both fear and gratitude. He would thank at times the very power he feared. But he also created Gods directly in his own image by the simple process of deifying his ancestors. Once he believed that his ancestors still existed as spirits they were only different from invisible Gods in degree. It was easy to take the next step and raise an ancestor to the rank of an actual God.

There are innumerable ways of making Gods and Goddesses. They are created out of man's needs and passions, his fancies and his blunders, his fears and his hopes. It would have been strange if he had never made them also out of his reverent and affectionate memory of his own predecessors. Round these elders and ancestors, men formed their first fundamental notions of right and duty and obedience. Consequently it was inevitable that religious and ethical ideas should be combined.

The process of manufacturing Gods goes back beyond the religion of "the family and the hearth" to the nomadic period. A primitive horde was likely to have a Horde-Ancestor-God; else why should the Greeks speak of their family Gods, Gods of their blood, paternal Gods and gentile Gods? In the Aryan horde it was natural that elders should make themselves respected and that the authority of lost fathers and mothers would be missed. There was no way in which early man could conceive of a providential or punitive deity except in terms of the punitive and providential practice of elders towards juniors, or of chiefs and patriarchs towards groups, or in terms of the action of hostile groups or persons. And so the primitive mind conceived an abstract divine judge, lawgiver and avenger, invoked to sanction the codes or customs of the elders or the patriarchs.

Tribal ethic progressively molded tribal religion and was in turn molded by it. It was not that man was incapable of forming moral ideas, as such, apart from religion. What happened was a mutual interaction of the norms of conduct. Theism would help the king; and monarchy would help theism. As a result the entire ethic of the community received a religious shape from which rational criticism could only gradually deliver it.

POLITICAL FACTORS

The view that religion arose from primitive ignorance of the working of nature is, of course, denied by those who believe that when the superstitious elements are purged a vital truth remains. It is often said that whatever may be the case with early religions, the higher developments are due to the genius of a gifted few. But we shall misread history if we think that a higher form of morality or religion could have been easily imposed on the mass of people. Nothing would be harder to accomplish. There is, I think, no known case of a flourishing priesthood reforming its own cult in the sense of willingly making an important change on moral lines. Akhenaton of Egypt, with all his autocratic power, failed to impose his monotheism on the nation. He was resisted by a powerful priesthood whose bread was buttered on the side of polytheism.

The sort of reform sometimes initiated by priesthoods is where a priest himself had been the subject of sacrifice, but the change merely consisted of laying the burden on others. In antiquity human sacrifices were sometimes suppressed by kings, but never by priesthoods. King Eurypylus is associated with the abolition of human sacrifice to Artemis Triclaria; Cecrops with the substitution of cakes for living victims to Zeus Lycaeus; Iphicrates and Gelon with the attempt to stop human sacrifices at Carthage. In Japan, at about the beginning of the Christian era, an Emperor introduced the substitution of clay images for servants who were formerly buried alive at the funeral of their prince. Similar cases are recorded in ancient China and elsewhere.

Whenever religious reformers try to bring about some important change, their chief problem is to persuade rulers or priests and fellow-worshippers that the move is desirable. Genius for management is fully as important as genius for righteousness. In an old cult a bald command to forgo, or reverse, an established rite would be bewildering to the worshippers. One way of making it acceptable is to invent a new myth. For example, it was the custom among the early Hebrews to sacrifice the firstborn of a man as well as of animals. The myth of Abraham and Isaac supplied a plausible pretext for making the change generally acceptable.

For the explanation of religious evolution, then, we must look not so much to genius for right thought as to genius for satisfying the common taste, or for outmaneuvering rival cults. By far the clearest case of cult or creed-shaping by a single genius is that of Mohammed. But it was the political expansion of Islam at a critical moment of history that made the fortunes of the faith, not the rise of the faith that made the fortunes of the Moslems. Had the Saracens not overrun the enfeebled Christian empire when Mohammedanism emerged, the new religion might have been no more than an obscure tribal worship.

What sharply defined Moselm dogma was the sense of triumphant opposition to Christian tritheism and Mary-worship. Once a religion has its sacred book, its tradition of triumph, and its established worship, the conservatism of the religious instinct counts for more in preserving it than the measure of genius that went to making it. Every religion, of course, sees supreme genius, both literary and religious, in its own Bible. No Christian can have a stronger conviction of the splendor of his sacred books than the Moslem enjoys concerning the Koran, the Brahmin over the Vedas, or the Buddhist in respect of the large literature of his system. But the progress of a religious system is largely determined by political and social factors.

THE GOD OF THE JEWS

The nominal monotheism of the Hebrews in Palestine, for example, was established by a political process. So was the polytheism in other States. All tribes and cities tended to worship a god who was the "Luck" of the community. He was nameless at first, but as an ancestor he often acquired a generic name. Other deities were added when tribes intermarried and the foreign women brought the deities of their own clan to form a pantheon. The ferocious myths of the Hebrews tell amply of the anxiety felt by the priests of Yahweh over this natural drift. They did their utmost to resist it, but the history of the Jews down to the Captivity shows their utter failure.

All the early Palestinian tribes tended to be monotheistic and polytheistic in the same way. When tribes coalesced and founded a city, a chief god was provided by the chief cult of the paramount tribe. Yahweh (or Yah, or Yaha) was simply a local worship aggrandized by the king and imposed on the fictitious history of the Hebrews long afterwards. There is overwhelming testimony to the boundless polytheism of the mass of people even in Jerusalem, the special seat of Yahweh, just before the Captivity. Monotheism did not really gain a hold in the sacred city until a long series of political pressures and convulsions had built up a special fanaticism for one cult. It represented the ethic of a priesthood seeking its own ends.

The main thesis of the prophetic and historical books of the Bible is that Yahweh is the God of Israel, and that Israel's sufferings are a punishment for worshipping other gods. All the troubles of the nation are seen as the result of departing from sole worship of the tribal god. When Jeremiah proclaims that "the showers have been withheld" by "the Lord that giveth rain" he is on the intellectual level of any tribal medicine-man. If those who held that doctrine understood all it entailed they would have been below the intellectual and moral level of the polytheists around them. For it implied that the one God desired the devotion of Israel alone, leaving all the other peoples to the worship of chimeras.

Monotheism of this type is in any case morally lower than polytheism since those who held it lacked sympathy with their neighbors. It seems to have arisen out of an angry refusal to say what the earlier Yahwists *had* said and believed: namely, that other nations had Gods, like Israel.

Most of the Jewish kings were polytheists. Monotheism grew out of this polytheism. There is absolutely no known case of a monotheism which did not emerge in a people who normally admitted the existence of a multitude of Gods.

What I am concerned to challenge is the assumption—due to the influence of Christianity—that Jewish monotheism is essentially higher than polytheism, and constitutes a great advance in the progress of religion. The usual reasons for this view are (1) that monotheism forbade images of God to be fashioned and so rejected idolatry; (2) that the Hebrew prophets expressed higher ethical ideals than those of the majority of ancient peoples at the time; (3) that the sexual code of the Hebrews was purer than that of their neighbors.

It is true that no representations of Yahweh were allowed. But the gain seems slight when we recall that this God was conceived in anthropomorphic terms with a local place of residence. The God of the pre-exilic Hebrews treated all strangers as outside his providence. If the mere affirmation of a Supreme

Creator God is taken to be a mark of superiority, certain primitive tribes who hold this doctrine and yet practice human sacrifice must be considered to have a "higher" religion than the late Greeks and Romans.

We need not suppose, on the other hand, that the great polytheistic states of Egypt and Babylon were *more* ethically advanced than the Hebrews, though in one important respect their polytheism had an advantage. Of its very nature it encouraged religious tolerance. When city was added to city, kingdom to kingdom, by conquest, the Gods of the defeated peoples were usually absorbed. Whole populations could not be driven out of one worship to another. As a sense of national unity arose the priesthoods of the capitals were obliged to accept the Gods of the outlying peoples.

It is a mere uncritical convention to regard the preservation of the Hebrew creed as a gain to civilization equal to the Greek victory over the invading Persians. To appraise rival cults rationally we must estimate their service either to ethics or to science and philosophy. By this criterion the religion of the Jews seems tribal, trivial, narrow. It remained tribalist and localist until the final fall of Jerusalem. It was a gospel of racial privilege and a practice of barbaric sacrifice—a law of taboo and punctilio, proclaiming a God of ritual and ceremonial, dwelling unseen in his chosen house, with much concern about its furniture and commissariat.

The protests occasionally made about the prevailing corruption only draw attention to the actual state of affairs. After the exile, the Hebrew attitude to sex is admittedly more refined than that of the licentious worship of other nations. This may have resulted from their struggle against the competition of neighboring cults. But it did not bring about an improvement in the status of women. Not only was vice as prevalent as elsewhere, but the Hebrew code of divorce was iniquitous. The law for the special punishment of women offenders remained at least formally barbarous down to the Christian era.

There can be no doubt that the Jewish exiles learned a great deal from their sojourn in Babylon. And it is highly probable that if Cyprus had not conquered Babylon, Hebrew "monotheism" might have disappeared. Even so, it tended to develop in the direction of dualism under the influence of the Babylonian and Persian doctrine of "the Adversary." The belief in angels and evil spirits was common throughout the East and amounted in the case of the Jews to a disguised polytheism. It is hard to see that the doctrine of the tyranny of a Supreme God over hosts of angels, with a rebel party included, is morally superior to the feudal family oligarchy of Olympus.

The Jews certainly put a greater distance between God and angels than the Mesopotamians, but there is little difference in the state of mind. It is, however, significant that the beginnings of rational science and ethics were not made by the Hebrew monotheists, but by the Babylonian and Greek polytheists. The latter went far in cosmic and moral philosophy, whereas the post-exilic Jews remained devotees of a God whose passionate and capricious will took the place of natural law.

SEEDS OF CHRISTISM

Persian overlordship in the Middle East was followed by the Macedonian; and Greek culture finally penetrated Syrian life in all directions. So far did the assimilation go that the Jewish hierarchy was faced by a Hellenising party, convinced of the futility of the old tribal religion. The zealots of Jerusalem were provoked beyond endurance. As a result the Maccabean revolt led to the reestablishment of a State in which the king was priest, just as previously the priest had been king. In the stress of this struggle we find the belief in the coming of the Messiah already so far developed that it amounts to the creation of a secondary God. The Christ of the Book of Enoch is substantially a God: "Before the sun and the signs were created, before the stars of heaven were made, his name was called before the Lord of the Spirits." He is at once Chosen One, Son of God and Son of Man; he is the judge at the Day of Judgment. As the Son of Woman he clearly relates to the Babylonian myth in the Book of Revelation. And seeing that in him dwells the spirit of Wisdom he is in effect at once the *Sophia* and the *Logos* of the Apocrypha and the Platonising Philo.

As the Jewish State came more and more into the whirl of battling empires, the king-priests passed away. Hellenism gained ground and once more the tribal faith was being disintegrated. One of the movements that appeared—though it did not originate—at this time is the cult associated with the quasi-historic name of Jesus (or Joshua). The central feature of the cult as it appears in the oldest document is the eucharist. This institution was common to many surrounding religions and known to have been in ancient and secret usage among sections of the Jews. Descending perhaps from totemistic times it invariably followed some rite or symbolism of eating a divine victim. The sacrificed God-man was the natural mythical complement of the ritual.

An actual historic person may or may not have been connected with the doctrine. There is, for example, the elusive figure of a Jesus who appears to have been put to death by stoning or hanging about a century before the death of Herod. On the other hand, the name in its Hebrew and Aramaic forms had probably an ancient divine status, being borne by the mythical Deliverer, Joshua, and again by the quasi-Messianic high-priest of the Restoration.

The oldest documents and tradition show that the cult of Jesus the Christ was being pushed in rivalry to pure Judaism among the Jews of the Dispersion before the destruction of the temple. Such competition was the more easy because the life of the synagogue was largely independent of the central temple and craved for rites and teaching which should make up for the sacrificial usages at Jerusalem.

As long as the temple stood, the main cult of the establishment could not be displaced. But in the existence of rival cults, especially those associated with the legendary Joshua, we can detect the seeds of ideas and practices which gave rise to Chistism. The name Jesus itself is a variant of Joshua (Jeschu), and the latter is an ancient deity reduced to human status. The Jews of the Hellenistic period regarded him as the actual founder of the rite of circumcision. According to tradition he began his work of deliverance on the day fixed for the choosing of the paschal lamb and concluded it at the Passover. The hypothesis that Joshua is the original Jesus—the origin of the myths which blended in a composite pattern mistaken for real history—solves many problems.

Jewish literature shows some striking instances of the development of polytheistic ideas which had been in existence for centuries. To the Good Spirit of Nehemiah, and the Logos or Word, was added the personified Sophia of the books of Proverbs and Ecclesiasticus and Enoch. The Samaritans seem to have conceived of a female Holy Spirit, symbolized, like several gods and goddesses, by a dove. The Jews who had come into contact with Greek thought developed the Eastern notion of the Logos into a new Jewish deity. They were so anxious to avoid goddess-worship that they represented God as generating the Son out of himself.

The association of Joshua with conceptions of Logos, Son of God, and Messiah is present in the Pentateuch. Joshua and the "Angel" (Mal'ak) of Yahweh, who was promised in Exodus to drive out enemy nations, are one and the same being, and from the statement that Yahweh's name is "in the Angel" we may infer that Yahweh himself was taken to be fighting under a human form. Moreover, the Talmud identifies the "Angel" with the mystical figure of Metatron, who is in turn a form of the Logos.

We shall consider the Logos doctrine in more detail later. Joshua is, as it were, the meeting point of ideas which came together long before Christianity. The name of Jesus (-Joshua) was revered in some quarters of Palestine and played much the same part in the Jewish liturgy for the ecclesiastical New Year as the Judaic Jesus in the Apocalypse on the Day of Judgment.

THE MAKING OF SECONDARY GODS

This brief survey of the evolution of religious ideas shows that they change their pattern by the same laws. Despite the aversion to change it cannot be resisted. God-making is a universal process, and the various lines of development are due to different environments. Under a professed monotheism we find the polytheistic tendency still at work, giving rise to the idea of a secondary god—the Logos, the Sophia, the Holy Spirit, the Christ. Jewish monotheism would have followed the same course but for the violent rupture that took place with Christism.

The subsequent record of Jewish monotheism does not support

the claim that it made for a higher life. It passed on no moralizing or unifying conception of life, for it had none to give. When we contemplate the mass of its ceremonial law, the endless complex of taboo, sacrifice and superstition we can but say that if men were good under such a regimen it was in spite of it, not in virtue of it.

Those Jews who sought a more idealistic religion turned hopefully to the new, breakaway movement of the Christists. From this movement a new, secondary god had emerged by the same process as elsewhere. The relation of the new god to the old was that of Son to Father.

Gods survive insofar as they are able to be adapted to new needs and conditions. In the orthodox Christian trinity the Holy Spirit has been from first to last a failure, technically speaking. For practical purposes the Holy Spirit was superseded by the Virgin Mother, and for philosophical purposes it merged with the Logos on the one hand, and with the Father-God on the other. Just as Jesus tended to supersede Yahweh, Mary in large measure tended to supersede Jesus and play the part of Mediator. There are even traces in medieval art of an attempt to make Mary's mother, Saint Anne, take the place of the Father in a new trinity. A similar tendency to create a secondary trinity out of Joseph, Mary and Jesus is not yet exhausted.

Christ-making is but a stage of god-making, the Christs or Son-Gods being secondary Gods. They are necessarily evolved out of prior material—the material of primitive cults to which men reverted in times of distress when they despaired of help from the Gods in nominal power. The old material is transformed and the result is a new god with fresh vitality through contact with the primary sources of religious emotion. He is turned to the account of new phases of emotion and moral need.

For example, in the Hellenised cult of the Thracian Bacchus, out of the very riot of savagery, the reek of blood and the living flesh torn by the hands and teeth of wine-maddened Maenads, there arises the dream of absorption in the God, and of utter devotion to his will, just as we meet it in the suicide-seeking transports of the early Christians. And even such a mystery as Hellenic hands wrought out of the hypostasis of the Beer-god, Hellenistic hands could shape from that of a man of sorrows, molding from the somber figure of the human sacrifice, slain a million times through aeons of ignorance, a God of another and more enduring cast.

In the understanding of this secondary process lies the comprehension of the history of "culture religion" as distinguished from the "nature religion" studied by anthropologists. With the typical secondary Gods, anthropology ends and hierology begins. But it is essential to a scientific view to remember that there has been no break in the evolution, no supernatural interposition. This will be sufficiently clear when we study the evolution of the secondary God in more detail.

Chapter Two

THE SACRIFICED SAVIOR GOD

The sacrifice of human beings, which was once widespread, took many different forms. Sometimes the victims were prisoners of war, sometimes they were the slaves or wives of a chief. In either case they were given a task to carry out in the spirit world. The captives were thought to appease the spirits of those killed in the fighting. Slaves and wives were sent to serve their dead master as they did on earth. Strictly speaking these killings are not quite the same as ritual sacrifice, when the victim is offered as a thanksgiving for victory or to propitiate an angry God. The common factor is the belief that some benefit will result from the sacrifice—either to the community or to an eminent individual. When the victim himself is believed to be a God—even though he may also be a scapegoat—we are dealing with an act of ritual magic.

The most remarkable of the man-god slaying cults which has been actually observed by anthropologists is that of the Khonds. They are a mountain people living in Orissa and they practiced human sacrifice as late as the mid-nineteenth century. They worshipped a Supreme Creator known as Boora Pennu. Under him were Tari Pennu, the Earth-Goddess, and second-class deities of rain, vegetation, hunting, war, boundaries, etc. Next came the deified, sinless men of the first age of the creation, and finally a multitude of local spirits.

Not all the Khond tribes indulged in human sacrifice. Those who did so made their offerings to Tari. They acknowledged theoretically that she was inferior to Boora, but they addressed their chief devotion to her. The Boora worshippers abhorred human sacrifice and believed it had been adopted under monstrous delusions devised by Tari who intended the final destruction of her followers. According to the myths Boora tried to prevent human sacrifice and on one occasion miraculously substituted a buffalo for a man. The explanation of the schism may well be that the sacrificial cult was originally taken over by a section of the Khonds from a race they conquered. It was from this apparently subject race that the human victims were obtained.

There was no shortage of supply. The *meriah*, which is one of the names given to the victim, was either bought or bred from an hereditary family set apart for the purpose. By the act of sacrifice the *meriah* became a God. In times of famine Khonds would willingly sell their own children so that they could meet this honorable death. The *meriah* had unlimited sexual liberty. His wife was also a destined victim, and the mother of victims to come.

The purpose of the rite was mainly to promote agricultural fertility, though it could be performed as a propitiation when some calamity occurred which seemed to indicate divine displeasure. The special religious and ethical feature was the belief that unless the victim was a volunteer he (or she) must be "bought with a price" and die for all mankind and not merely for the Khonds.

The rite lasted three or five days. On the first day the *meriah's* head was shaved and the people spent the night in licentious revels. The next day he was bathed and newly clothed and taken to a sacred grove. Tied to a stake, he was anointed with oil and turmeric, garlanded with flowers and worshipped. Another night of debauchery followed. In the final stage a specially instructed priest officiated in a manner which leaves no doubt about the religious nature of the ceremony. The priest must be a celibate whose austerity is paraded. He has gained sanctity through personal uncleanliness. His primary function is to brave the curse of the sacrificed and deified victim. On the one hand, the victim reproaches his slayers while avowing that by their act he is made a God; and on the other hand, the priest and the headman defend themselves by pointing out that the *meriah* was purchased and dedicated, and that he consented to this role as a child.

Finally he was either fastened to a cross of which the horizontal bar, pierced by the upright, could be raised or lowered at will; or alternatively placed in the cleft branch of a green tree, which was made to grasp his neck or chest. The effect was to imprison him in the wood so that he himself was virtually the upright of a cross. One of the most significant acts in the entire ritual occurred at this stage. It was essential that the victim should not finally resist. To make sure his arms and legs were broken and he could be made passive by drugs. The priest then slightly wounds him with an axe and the crowd instantly cuts him to pieces, leaving only the head and intestines untouched. These are subsequently burned and the ash spread over the fields or laid as a paste on houses and granaries. Portions of the flesh were solemnly carried to the participating villages and distributed to the people for burial in the fields.

The rite varied in detail according to the district. The most humane form was to drug the victim with opium or datura before leading him to the place of execution. Sometimes, however, the priest followed an opposite principle in the belief that the infliction of pain made the sacrifice more efficacious. It was thought that the Earth goddess would supply rain in proportion to the quantity of tears extracted. The manner of death also differed. Victims were stoned, beaten to death with tomahawks or heavy iron rings, strangled, crushed. Sometimes the priest plunged a wooden image into the gaping wound so that the mannikin might be gorged with blood. All that is constant is the principle of a redemptory bloody sacrifice.

When the Khonds were persuaded to end human sacrifices they substituted a buffalo and treated it with much the same ritual. A similar substitution is recorded at the Dassara festival in Jeypore where a ram was decapitated after it had been clothed and seated like a human being. This enables us to credit the statement in the *Satapatha Brahmana* that "in the beginning the sacrifice most acceptable to the gods was man," and that "for the man a horse was substituted, then an ox, then a sheep, then a goat, until at length it was found that the gods were most pleased with offerings of rice and barley." The progression from man to animals has repeatedly occurred and it is impossible to explain such cases as survivals or revivals of totem sacrifices. It is reasonable to assume that the same evolution occurred in ancient Greece and elsewhere, at least in some of the surrogate sacrifices.

THE CHRISTIAN CRUCIFIXION

To those who have not realized how all religion evolved from savage beginnings, it will seem extravagant to suggest that the story of the Christian crucifixion was built up from practices such as those above described. And yet the grounds for inferring such a derivation are strong.

Frazer has drawn attention to the sacrifice of a mock-king in the Perso-Babylonian feast of Sacaea. He assumes that the crucifixion story is historical. The analogy with the mock-crowning and the scourging of Christ does not compel us to suppose that the latter was an actual event. There are other features which Frazer does not emphasize which provide important clues. Some of these are illuminated by the rite of the Khonds.

For instance, the Khonds placed their victim on a cross or on a cleft bough in such a way as to make a living cross. A no less suggestive parallel is the breaking of the victim's arms and legs to make him seem unresisting, and the substitution of opium as being less cruel. As far away as Mexico, in an annual festival to the Fire-god, the victims were painted red, like the Khond *meriah*, and a narcotic powder was thrown in their faces.The god was expressly represented by a tree, stripped of bark and branches, but covered with painted paper.

Let us now take the Christian parallels.

In the fourth Gospel we are told that after the death of Jesus, the Jews asked Pilate that the bodies should have their legs broken and be removed before the Sabbath. The soldiers broke the legs of the "two others" as they were not dead. Jesus was spared, his heart being pierced with a lance "that the Scripture might be fulfilled: a bone of him shall not be broken." The other gospels say nothing on this point, but all four tell of the offering of a drink.

In Matthew "vinegar mixed with gall" is offered beforehand and refused after tasting. A sponge of vinegar is offered apparently in sympathy after the cry of Eli, Eli. The Vulgate and Ethiopic versions, the Sinaitic, Vatican and Bezan codices, and many old MSS. read *wine* for vinegar, while the Arabic version reads myrrh for gall. In Mark the first drink becomes "wine spiced with myrrh" and it is refused without tasting. The commentators recognize that the purpose was presumably to cause stupefaction and so lighten suffering. In Luke this detail entirely disappears and the vinegar offered on the cross is given in mockery. In John also, only the drink offered on the cross is mentioned, and of this it is said, "When Jesus had received the vinegar he said 'It is finished.'" Then follows the detail as to the breaking of the legs.

What concerns us here is the source of the symbolism rather than the discrepancies. One compiler clearly knows of a drink offered before the crucifixion and implies that it was intended to cause euthanasia, for he notes that it was refused. The divine victim must be a conscious sufferer. A later compiler ignores this detail and notes only that the victim was tormented with a drink of vinegar. Both these details are un-Roman. The torment was trivial, while the narcotic would be inconsistent with what was meant to be exemplary punishment. The fourth gospel makes the victim accept the vinegar as the last symbolic act of sufferance, and then mentions the limb-breaking. The divine victim is exempted for dogmatic reasons, the fact of his death being made certain by a lance-thrust. The other compilers omit this detail. The author, or interpolator, of the fourth gospel, saw the need to make it clear that the bones of the Messiah remained unbroken. As a true paschal sacrifice it was important that the law as to the Passover should be fulfilled in the Messiah.

On what data, then, did the different evangelists proceed? Not an original narrative or they would not differ so much. Not a known official practice in Roman crucifixions, for the third gospel treats as an act of mockery what the first and second regard as one of mercy. The fourth gospel describes the limb-breaking as being done to meet a Jewish demand. Mere breaking of legs is an inadequate way of making sure that the victims were dead, compared with a spear thrust; yet only one victim is speared.

Only one hypothesis will meet the whole case. The different narratives testify to the existence of a ritual, or rituals, of crucifixion, or quasi-crucifixion. The two procedures for breaking the legs and giving a narcotic were variant forms. These procedures were not fully understood by the evangelists and their conflict is as insoluble as their testimony is unhistorical.

If the ritual of a crucified savior-god underwent a similar evolution in the Mediterranean world as we have seen among the Khonds, we have the conditions which may account for the varying gospel narratives. The story of the betrayal by Judas, incredible as it stands, is intelligible when seen as one more item of sacrificial practice. The Pauline phrase, "bought with a price" (i Cor. vi.20) ostensibly conveys the meaning of "ransomed" and is not applied to Jesus. But the paying of a price to Judas by the high priests would become quite intelligible as one more detail in a mystery drama growing out of a ritual of human sacrifice. "Judas" is presumably derived from *Joudaios*, a Jew, and the basis of the episode would be a Gentile imputation, thus understood, that the Jews sold the Lord as a human sacrifice. The doctrine put in the mouth of Caiaphas in the fourth gospel (xi.50–51) is a doctrine of human sacrifice.

VOGUE OF HUMAN SACRIFICE

What positive evidence have we for the existence of human sacrifice in the Mediterranean world about the beginning of the Christian era? There is no question about the prevalence of the ritual among more primitive peoples. Tribes in northern and eastern Europe at the time of their contact with the Romans are known to have sacrificed captives. There are many stories which show the existence in Greece of a primitive custom of sacrificing a human victim. Later this followed by the use of a surrogate, often an animal. A goat was substituted for a boy in sacrifice to Dionysus at Potniae, and a hart for a virgin at Laodicea. But King Athamas had been called upon to sacrifice his firstborn son by the Delphic oracle; Menelaos sacrificed two children in Egypt when stayed by contrary winds; three Persian boys were offered up at the battle of Salamis.

The sacrifice of children was at one time as normal among the Semites as among the ancient Mexicans and Peruvians. Such practices became more and more rare as civilization advanced, though they persisted in one or two places even in the Roman Empire. It was only in the time of Hadrian that the annual human sacrifice to Zeus was abolished at Salamis in Cyprus.

Strabo has described a ritual practiced by the primitive Albanians, who lived south of the Caucasian mountains and west of the Caspian. It corresponds in one notable detail to the gospel narratives. One of the sacred slaves of the high priest of the Moon-goddess would become divinely possessed and wander alone in the woods. He was then seized, bound with sacred fetters, and maintained sumptuously for a year. When the festival day came, he was anointed with a fragrant ointment, and slain by being pierced to the heart through the side with a sacred lance. So, too, in the annual spring festival at Salamis, the victim was led three times round the altar, and pierced by the priest with a lance, the corpse being finally burned on a pyre.

Tertullian's testimony brings us closer to civilization, though he is not the best of witnesses. When he says that children were secretly sacrificed in Carthage in his own day he is repeating a rumor that has not been investigated. But when he tells of children being publicly sacrificed to Saturn as late as the proconsulship of Tiberius, who thereupon crucified a number of priests on the sacred trees beside their temples, he is saying something that squares with a good deal of testimony about Semitic practices.

Hamilcar had sacrificed his own son at the siege of Agrigentum, 407 B.C. There is evidence of the annual sacrifice of a boy to Kronos at Tyre which was only given up when Alexander besieged the city. Among the Arabs it seems certain that human sacrifices were offered in the generation before Mohammed. We have no clear record of the date when human sacrifices ceased in the Thurgelia festival at Athens. It is probable that these merged into the ritual execution of a criminal. There is no ground for thinking that any Athenian would wince at putting a criminal to death by religious rites. Such usages may have continued long after the Periclean age, though they were no longer *called* human sacrifices.

Just as the sacrifice of human beings became so repugnant that various types of surrogates took their place, so the primitive cannibalism associated with it was refined by the substitution of animal flesh, bread and cakes. Because the early ritual was essentially religious the sacrifice had a sacramental character. The primordial victim was believed to be divine. This is a reasonable inference from many myths when we realize that myths are often invented long after the rites which they pretend to explain.

Thus the legends concerning the Titans and the birth, death and rebirth of Dionysus, explain the sacrifice of a boy at Potniae, and the later substitution of a goat. Originally the boy, later the animal, were eaten as a means of communion with the God. Again, the Sinaitic Arabs of the fourth century substituted a young white camel for a human victim. The blood of the camel was drunk by the tribesmen, and the animal was cut to pieces and instantly devoured raw. There is strong evidence that the human victim was normally eaten by primitive peoples, as it was by the semi-civilized Mexicans at the time of the Spanish conquest. Cannibalism has been practiced in all parts of the world and it persisted in its religious form long after it ceased to be a normal practice. The recoil from cannibalism which marks the rise of humanity would lead in the more civilized states to the setting apart of criminals, on the one hand, and the substitution of animals on the other, for sacrifice. The surrogates would be regarded as a representative and incarnation of the God and at the same time serve for the typical sacramental meal.

A difficulty must be faced, however, in the case of criminals. It was an almost universal rule among the higher races of antiquity that the victim must be pure and without blemish. A criminal would seem to be the last man to suit the part. But the idea of what constitutes fitness varies considerably. In primitive communities the act of execution constantly assumes a sacrificial character. Criminals were regarded much in the same way as prisoners of war, and their use as substitutes may well have grown out of the earlier custom of sacrificing captives. Caesar records that the Gauls considered those who had committed theft or other crimes "more grateful to the immortal Gods," and that when the supply ran short "they descended to sacrifices of the innocent." Needless to say, the simple recoil in more civilized periods from wilful sacrifice of the innocent would encourage the resort to victims under sentence of death.

Porphyry states that a condemned prisoner was selected for the annual sacrifice of a man to the ancient Semitic deity Kronos at Rhodes. The prisoner was led outside the city gates and having been given wine to drink was put to death. Here we have a parallel in the Mediterranean world to a typical detail in the gospel mystery play. The Kronian victim cannot have been originally a criminal. It is much more likely that he originally personated either the god Kronos or his "only begotten son," Ieond, whom, in a Phoenician myth, Kronos is said to have sacrificed after dressing him in royal robes.

We may conclude, therefore, that when the necessity arose, the barbarian mind felt no difficulty in making the transition to a criminal for sacrifice. Moreover, when an animal was substituted, reasons for eating it could readily be found by worshippers who made myths out of misunderstood survivals of totemism. The worshippers of Dionysus could feel that they were commemorating the dismemberment of the god when they ate the raw flesh of a bull or a kid. And, granted that such modifications took place, we have to reckon with the tendency noticeable throughout religious history to revert to some archaic rite in times of national disaster or uncertainty.

EATING THE GOD

The Romans resorted to eastern and Egyptian Gods in times of desperate war. Magical rites multiply in decaying civilizations. In every age we find a reversion to fortune-telling in periods of stress. And the *idea* of religious anthropophagy certainly prevailed in the early Christian world. The formulae: "Take, eat, this is my body" and "Drink ye all of it, for this is my blood" cannot conceivably be other than adaptations from a mystery ritual in which a sacrificed God spoke by the mouth of his priests.

In the fourth gospel the act of symbolical theophagy is amplified so that it is made a means to immortality. "I am the bread of life . . . I am the living bread which came down from heaven: if any man eat of this bread he shall live for ever: yea, and the bread which I will give is my flesh, for the life of the world . . . Except ye eat the flesh of the Son of Man and drink his blood ye have not life in yourselves. He that eateth my flesh and drinketh my blood hath eternal life; and I will raise him up at the last day. For my flesh is true meat, and my blood is true drink. He that eateth my flesh and drinketh my blood abideth in me and I in him." (John, vi. 48–56.)

The eucharist, both in the myth and in the nature of the cult, stands in the closest relation to the act of human sacrifice. For the compilers of the fourth gospel the Crucified One is the final and universal paschal sacrifice. He was slain at the time of the paschal lamb-eating, whereas in the synoptics he had previously partaken of the sacrifice. That this conception existed before the gospels were written is clear from the book of Revelation where Jesus is identified with the Alpha and Omega (i.e. the Almighty) and at the same time with "the Lamb that was slain."

In the gospel the God must found his own eucharist before his death. Since the victim is himself, the God eats of his own flesh. It is doubtless by way of refining upon the earlier practice of flesh eating that in the synoptics the God is made to call the bread his flesh. In the course of the supper he presumptively ate the prescribed flesh of his special symbol and representative, the lamb. There are parallels in the mysteries of Mithra, the mystical eucharist of the Egyptians, the cult of Dionysus. In many Christian churches there was an ancient custom of sacrificing and eating an actual lamb. When that ceased a baked image of the lamb was substituted. There were two views of the eucharist in the early Church. One regarded the ritual of the Holy Supper as purely mystical; the other, a realistic view, is founded on the whole historical analogy of sacrifice which meant a communion with the God in partaking a common meal.

This pattern of sacramental sacrifice would seem to be primordial. It is associated with the idea of resurrection which developed as a doctrine of personal immortality from the primary conception of the annual revival of vegetation. It became part of the mystery rituals of Osiris and Dionysus, and of the Eleusinia, long before the Christian era. What we must now investigate is how this ancient rite could have given rise to the crucifixion story.

One theory is that the gospel myth derives some of its details from an ancient Babylonian New Year festival via the Jewish feast of Purim. Frazer has pointed out the resemblance between the mockery endured by Jesus and the ritual of the Sacaea which the exiled Jews must have become acquainted with in Babylon.

The Babylonians celebrated the Sacaea by putting to death a malefactor who masqueraded as king, wearing a crown and royal robe before being hanged or crucified. It is not intrinsically unlikely that the fast which precedes the Purim was, in Babylon, a ceremonial mourning for a God who died like Tammuz or Adonis and rose again on the third day. But there is the difficulty that the Purim occurred earlier than the Passover, and though this is not in itself insurmountable, a more serious objection is that there are important details in the crucifixion story which are as alien to the Purim as they are cognate with the paschal rite. And Frazer, as we have noted, assumes that the crucifixion is a matter of history, not mythology. Precisely because he has shown that the practice of human sacrifice to the vegetation or God was so nearly universal it is not necessary to suppose that the Jews owed their variant solely to late contact with another nation. It is more likely that the crucifixion myth is partly drawn from an old Semitic rite resembling the Sacaea in some features and known in Palestine in a simpler form before the exile. It is to the Passover rather than the Purim that we must turn. For the memory of human sacrifice is clearly stamped on the Passover.

Chapter Three

PAGAN SURVIVALS IN JUDAISM

Among the aspects of the gospel story which the analogy of the Babylonian Sacaea leaves untouched are (1) mourning for the victim, (2) his alleged divinity and titles of Son of God and Son of Man, (3) his participation in a sacramental meal in which his flesh is mystically eaten, (4) his execution along with two criminals, (5) his resurrection, (6) his subsequent status as Messiah or Christos. The first four have an evident connection with the paschal rite. There is no need to look beyond the Passover to the Purim for an actual killing of royal victims or malefactors at a sacrificial festival. The legend of the hanging of the seven sons of Saul "before the Lord," happened, we are told, at the barley festival—i.e. at the time of the Passover. The rite itself was originally a sacrifice of firstborn children, and the conflict or laws on the subject suggests that the later substitution of animal offerings was made with difficulty.

That the hanging of Saul's sons was an act of propitiation

can be gathered from the remark "after that God was entreated for the land." Also the expressions "before the Lord" and "unto the Lord" mean sacrifice or nothing. Equally sacrificial, though the usual formula is not applied to it, was the hanging of the five kings of Joshua in the pseudo-history. The procedure is the same in Joshua's hanging of the King of Ai. We are explicitly told in the Hebrew that he "devoted" all the people of Ai, as he had done those of Jericho. As Ai is an imaginary city we must conclude that the legend points to a customary rite.

The Greek word *anathema* has the double meaning of "devoted" and "accused." A passage in Deuteronomy states that every hanged man bears "the curse of God." This has the same meaning as "devoted to God." in the Book of Joshua. Exactly the same procedure is followed in both cases: the hanged victim is taken down and buried within the day.

All hanged men in ancient Jewry were sacrifices to the Sun-god or Rain-god. It may be taken as historically certain that human sacrifice in this aspect was a recognized part of Hebrew religion until the Exile. As on so many other points there are parallels among other primitive peoples.

Hanging is not to be construed in the narrow sense of death by strangulation. The normal method of ancient "crucifixion" was hanging by the wrists. Animal victims were hanged to a tree in the cult of the Syrian goddess in the second century of our era. Human victims were bound or hanged to trees in the sacrificial rites of the ancient Mexicans. Human sacrifices to Odin and other Teutonic deities were often hanged. It is significant that among the early Odin-worshippers, as among the Greeks and Semites, the king's sons were often substituted for their fathers, though latterly their place was taken by slaves and criminals. In some of the Scandinavian cases, the victim was wounded with a javelin as well as hanged.

The late myths of Abraham and Isaac and of the Exodus were employed to effect the change from child to animal sacrifice. It was at this stage, presumably, that the practice began of breaking the victim's limbs, and later of drugging them to prevent the struggles which were held to make a sacrifice inauspicious. The manner in which the caveat against breaking the bones of the paschal lamb is introduced indicates that it was either a late provision against a practice that recalled the rite of human sacrifice, or a specific assertion of the principle that the victim must be without blemish, which drugging or maiming would have violated.

ANIMAL SUBSTITUTES

The clues afforded by the many parallels between sacrificial rites throughout the world suggest the following line of evolution:

1. Originally it was necessary for the victim to be willing. Cooperation was secured by the bribe of a period of luxurious living and sexual license.
2. When this type of victim became hard to procure, one was "bought with a price." He represented a voluntary offering by those who owned him.
3. To give a semblance that the victim was a willing sacrifice, his limbs were broken so that he could not struggle.
4. When it came to be felt that such a mangled victim was unseemly, he was drugged with a narcotic.
5. At a higher stage of social evolution there was a recoil from the idea of sacrificing an innocent victim. Resort was had to condemned criminals, and these were usually stupefied.
6. Finally objections were felt to a stupefied victim. Such a non-suffering sacrifice seemed unseemly or inefficacious. Accordingly an animal substitute was found. In certain cases the animal was given human attributes; in others it received some of the privileges formerly accorded to the taboo human victim. It was not as a rule thought necessary to break bones or give a narcotic to an animal. The reformers would stress the avoidance of bone-breaking to emphasize the superiority of the new sacrifice. Hence the need for a veto on imitations of the old practice.

In addition to the Passover there are two other Jewish feasts which bear traces of original human sacrifice: the sacrifice of the Red Heifer, said to have been performed only eight times since Moses, and that of a scapegoat on the Day of Atonement.

The Red Heifer rite was prescribed to take place on the Mount of Olives. The High Priest, his eldest son and the Messiah Milchama—the deputy High Priest anointed for war—were all three anointed with oil and the mark of a cross was made on their foreheads. According to one account a pregnant woman was kept in a temple chamber until her child was born. It was brought up in the sacred precincts and so kept from pollution. During the rite the child was seated on a wooden litter and borne by bullocks to the fountain of Siloah. The child descended and drew water from the spring in an earthen vessel. It was then conducted back to the Temple. In another version more than one pregnant woman were kept in the courts built on the rock, with an excavation underneath. They and their children were kept there "for the use of the red heifer" until the children were seven or eight years old, when they ceased to be held ceremonially pure.

It is fairly clear that a regular supply of child victims had been anciently provided for the sacrifice, and that the heifer was the child's representative. There is a dubiously significant saying in the Talmud that "as the red heifer atones for sin so also does the death of the righteous atone for sin." Being sacrificed with her face to the south and her head to the west, the heifer was presumably dedicated either to the setting or winter sun, or to the Moon-goddess.

SCAPEGOAT AS SIN-OFFERING

The ritual of the sacrifice of the scapegoat also provides a clue to its original character. The High Priest was removed from his house to the council chamber seven days in advance, and a deputy was appointed in case he should become incapacitated.

On the night before the sacrifice he was not allowed to eat meat or to sleep; he was watched by the younger priests. The elders of the Sanhedrin then handed him over to the seniors of the priestly order who swore him in. In administering the oath they said, "My lord high priest we are ambassadors of the Sanhedrin, and *thou art ambassador of the Sanhedrin and our ambassador also*. We adjure thee by Him who causes his name to dwell in this house, that thou deviate not from anything we have rehearsed to thee. Then they parted company, *both he and they weeping*."

It is sufficiently clear that the rite was originally one of human sacrifice in which either the priest or his deputy was put to death as ambassador of the people to God, or the Gods—that is, as a scapegoat for their sins. In all likelihood the Hebrews practiced some form of this rite long before the Captivity. And as regards the later, modified practice there is a significant Talmudic clue in the saying of Rabbi Eleazar that it is lawful to slay an *Amhaaretz* (one ignorant of the law, a rustic pagan) on the Day of Atonement when it falls on the Sabbath. It is further explained that the victim must not be slain with a knife as this would require a formal benediction; but to kill him by tearing his nostrils open no benediction is necessary. According to another Rabbi it is lawful to split up the *Amhaaretz* like a fish.

The modified sacrifice of the scapegoat, then, was but another variant of the primordial principle of human sacrifice or "sin-offering" for the good of the people, and is in many respects the complement of the Passover. The Passover was set apart on the tenth day of the civil New Year, which dated from spring; the Day of Atonement was the tenth day from the ecclesiastical New Year, which began in autumn. It is probable that the latter is the older of the two; but both hold their ground in reference to the sun's progress, the spring festival standing for his youth and waxing period, the autumn for his maturity and waning. Both festivals had the sacrifice of a pure victim in common, as we can see from the fact that the victim was kept in an "upper chamber" beforehand to avoid contamination. And both festivals could be celebrated apart from the Temple. The Passover was a domestic as well as a temple feast; and the Day of Atonement was celebrated in Babylon as well as in Jerusalem.

Although Jewish sacrifices were strictly national, when they made contact with other races they were attracted towards more cosmopolitan ideals. The Gentilizing Christians founded their gospel on the concept of a sacrifice for the benefit of "mankind." We must note, too, the general belief that the sacrifice of a king's son, offered up for his father, was specially potent. Eusebius preserved a myth from Philo of Byblos that Kronos, "whom the Phoenicians call Israel," adorned his only son "Ieond" with emblems of royalty and sacrificed him. There is also the story of Maleus who crucified his only son, crowned and robed in purple before the walls of Carthage, in order to conquer the city.

Always it is the typically divine or racial "father"—Kronos, Israel, Abraham—who figures in myths of son-sacrifice. The name "Tammuz" signified "the son of life" in its original Akkadian form, and was interpreted by the Semites as "the offspring" or "only son." We may conclude from this that the god's death and resurrection had a strong hold on both non-Semitics and Semitic races. The Hebrew cult of the death and resurrection of Tammuz was carried on before the Exile in the very triumph of Yaweh.

PRE-CHRISTIAN CULT OF JESUS

The natural inference from the gospel story of Barabbas is that it was quite customary to give to the people about the time of the Passover a prisoner who was made to play a part in some rite under the name of Barabbas, "Son of the Father." We gather from Origen that "Jesus Barabbas" was the accepted reading of Matt. XXVII. 16.17 in the ancient Church. May we not presume that a "Jesus the Son of the Father" was a figure in an old Semitic ritual of sacrifice before the Christian era? The Syrian form of the name, Yeschu, closely resembles the Hebrew name Yishak (Isaac). It is fair to assume that Isaac, in an earlier myth, was sacrificed by his father; and that Abraham was originally a divine figure, like Israel.

There are various grounds for surmising a pre-Christian cult of a Jesus (or Joshua). He is quite certainly unhistorical. The Book of Joshua leads us to think that he had several attributes of the Sun-god, and that, like Samson and Moses, he was an ancient deity reduced to human status. This would explain why he is put on a level with Moses as an institution of the Passover rite and circumcision, and credited with the miracle of staying the course of the sun—a prodigy beyond any ascribed to Moses. In Exodus it is prophesied that an Angel in the name of Yaweh, would lead Israel to triumph against the Amorites, Hittites and Jebusites—the very list (lacking one) of the conquests effected by the Lord through Joshua. By virtue of his possession of the magical name he is identified in the Talmud with the mystic Metatron, who is in turn identified with the Logos. Thus the name Joshua-Jesus is already associated in the Pentateuch with conceptions of the Logos, Son of God and Messiah.

Further evidence can be found in the Apocalypse. The Jesus of that whole book is pre-Christian. It identifies the slain god with the Logos before the appearance of the Fourth Gospel, and with the Mithraic or Babylonian symbols of the Seven Spirits as well as with the Alpha and Omega. The Book of Revelations is in fact a Jewish Apocalypse slightly edited for Christian purposes. So, too, "The Teaching of the Twelve Apostles" is not a Christian but a Judaic document. The references it contains to "Jesus" are therefore pre-Christian.

The Messianic idea seems to have come to the Jews during their Exile, perhaps from the Old Babylonian myth of the return of Hammurabi who declared himself to be the Savior-Shepherd and the King of Righteousness. Another possible source might be the Mazdean doctrine that at the end of time the Savior Saoshyant, the yet unborn son of Zarathustra, would raise the dead and destroy Ahriman. Needless to say, any such associations would be obliterated by later Judaism.

What is specially important in this connection is the late development of the doctrine of a *suffering* Messiah. The New Testament assertion that the Christ must needs have suffered is only supported by passages like the fifty-third chapter of Isaiah where the Authorized Version alters the past tense into the present and makes a description of Israel's past suffering serve as a mystic type. The first clear trace of the conception of a suffering Messiah in Judaic literature is the doctrine that of the two promised Messiahs, Ben Joseph and Ben David, the former is to be slain. The most likely pagan prototype is the slain and resurgent Dionysus, one of whose chief names is Elenthereos, the Liberator. He is described as the God "born again."

As the Jewish Messiah was primarily a "Deliverer," like the national heroes in the Book of Judges, a popular God so designated would be most likely to impress the imagination of the dispersed Jews and their proselytes. To account for the revival of such conceptions after the Exile, we must look to the religious ideas that prevailed in the surrounding Hellenistic civilization, especially to the myths of Dionysus and Heracles, and the Son-sacrificing Kronos.

THE JEWISH EUCHARIST

The most likely places where the sacrificial cult we have been investigating would make contact with the Jews were the synagogues outside Judea. Wherever in the East there was a Jewish synagogue, there was an opening for usages not recognized at Jerusalem. Apart from the Passover there were no regular sacrificial rites for the expatriated Jews. It is likely enough that they would revive rites which had a great tradition behind them, but were not latterly practiced at the temple. The craving for a sacrifice in which they could participate is the special note of the Epistle to the Hebrews. It was far too deeply rooted for myriads of scattered Jews to submit contentedly to a complete deprivation of the practice.

Significantly enough, the most notable survival among the Jews in modern times is one that preserves the principle of human sacrifice. This is the slaying of a white cock on the eve of Yom Kippur, the Day of Atonement. An account of the rite as practiced by the Jews of Barbary in the seventeenth century states that the sacrifice came after the reading of the ancient Confession held to be made by the high priest in sacrificing the scapegoat. The formula used was: "Let this cock be a commutation for me. Let it be my substitute. Let it be an expiation for me. Let the bird die, but let life and happiness be to me and all Israel." The cock was then killed and eaten. In other places the cock is not eaten at the sacrifice but given to the poor.

I have seen an illustrated postcard made for German Jews in which a Jew in hat and long coat is depicted holding a white cock in front of a table with a book on it. Underneath is the Hebrew text, "Deliver him from going down to the pit: I have found a ransom." This is followed by greetings in German for the New Year. The fact that the sacrificer holds the tied legs of the bird in his right hand, while with his left on its head he coaxes it to keep quiet, recalls the old effort to secure the willing victim. The procedure includes a "ransom for the Kapparoth"—that is a ransom for the ransom, a principle familiar to the student of ancient sacrifice. Here the substitution of a lesser victim for human sacrifice is almost undisguised, after two thousand years.

There are parallels to the sacrifice of a white cock in Africa, India and Greece. As a surrogate for human sacrifice it was probably ancient among the Semites. By reviving such mysteries the Jews of the Dispersion could compensate themselves for being unable to take part in the rituals which were a monopoly of Jerusalem. When we find the later Christists practicing a rite analogous to those of Mithra and Dionysus, we cannot doubt that the Jews in the large eastern cities would be inclined to resort to mysteries of sacrament sacrifice. There were precedents in their own traditions. It is a Rabbinical doctrine that "so long as the Temple existed the altar made atonement for Israel; but now it is a man's table that makes atonement for him."

In the exilic period there had been many resorts to "unclean" sacraments, such as the mystical eating of dogs, mice and swine. But plenty of pretexts could be found in the sacred books for "clean" sacraments in honor of Yahweh. The essential notion in all orthodox sacrifices was that the worshipper could eat and drink with the deity, sitting at his table like a guest at a great banquet. This was the ideal for the laity as well as the priesthood. It would be strange indeed if the dispersed Jews wholly renounced such an experience.

How often would such a rite occur? In the later Jesuist cult, a weekly eucharist of bread and wine is connected with the sacrifice of the god. This relation is absent from the earlier form of the "Teaching of the Twelve Apostles," though the latter supports what we have other reasons for surmising—a long-standing weekly rite among the Jews of the Dispersion. It is certain that there was a weekly eucharist among the Mithraists, but this was only one of the ancient Asiatic usages which could reach the Jews by way of Babylon or even before the Captivity. The Hindus celebrated the sacrament of the Soma four times in each lunar month. Thus the first day of the week was a "Lord's Day" long before the Christian era. That the Sumerians or

Akkadians, who had a seven day week, were the source of the weekly bread and wine supper for both the Hindus and Persians seems a natural hypothesis.

The denunciations of the prophets against drink offerings to other gods did not veto a eucharist eaten and drunk in the name of Yahweh. Whether or not there is a precedent in the consumption of the sacred shew-bread of the temple on the Sabbath, there are many Gentile precedents for the eucharist. Its connection with the Lord's Day is quite independent of the gospel myth. The final association with the sacrifice of the God-man as king, and the kindred sacrament of the Lamb-God were derived from pagan sources through Judaic channels.

Chapter Four

ORIGINS OF THE GOSPEL MYTH

The evolution of the Jewish religion between the closing of the Hebrew canon and the rise of Jesuism consisted broadly in (1) the establishment of the doctrine of a future life, although it had been completely absent from the Mosaic law; (2) the development of the belief in a Messiah who should either restore the temporal power of Jewry or bring in a new religious world; (3) the growth of the idea of an only-begotten Son of God, otherwise the Word, who is alternately the nation of Israel and a God who represents it; (4) the growth of independent sects or movements such as the Essenes. Together with this we find a recurrent paganization of portions of the priesthood, an interlude of absolute pagan domination, and finally, after a period of triumph for the traditional faith, the advent of the Idumean dynasty, far from zealous for orthodox Judaism.

During centuries of this evolution, the Jewish people tasted many times the bitterness of despair and the profound doubt denounced by the last of the prophets. In periods when many went openly over to Hellenism, it could not but be that ancient rites of the Semitic race were revived, as some are declared to have been in earlier times of trouble. Among the rites of expiation and propititiation, none stood traditionally higher than the sacrifice of the king, or the king's son. The Jews saw such an act performed for them, as it were, when the Romans under Antony, at Herod's wish, scourged, crucified [lit. "bound to stake"], and beheaded Antigonous, the last of the Asmonean priest kings in 37 B.C. In a reign in which two king's sons were slain by their own father, the idea would not disappear; insofar as it held its ground as a religious doctrine, it would in all likelihood do so by being reduced to ritual form, like the leading worships of the surrounding Gentile world.

Nearly every god who mythically died and rose again—e.g. Osiris, Dionysus, Attis, Adonis and Mithra—was believed to have had the power to give immortal life. This creed was maintained by a ritual sacrament, generally developed into a mystery drama. At bottom the mystery drama was a perpetuation of the latest form of the primitive rite as it had been publicly performed. We have already noted a trace in the gospel myth of the ancient usage of disabling or drugging the victim to make him seem a willing sufferer. There are grounds for supposing that the latest public form of the human sacrifice in some Syrian communities was the public sacrifice of three criminals together.

The number three was of mystic significance in many parts of the East. The Dravidians of India sacrificed three victims to the Sun-god. In western as in eastern Asia, the number three would have its votaries in respect of trinitarian concepts as well as the primary notion of "the heavens, the earth and the underworld." Traditionally the Syrian rite called for a royal victim. The substitution of criminals for the king or king's son was repugnant, however, to the higher doctrine that the victim should be unblemished. To solve this problem one of the malefactors was distinguished from the other criminals by a ritual of mock-crowning and robing in the spirit of "sympathetic magic." By parading him as king, and calling the others what indeed they were, it was possible to attain the semblance of a truly august sacrifice.

The custom of permitting the chosen victim a year's licence was general among the Asiatics, Greeks, Polynesians, Mexicans and American aborigines. No such indulgence could have been accepted in the Christian legend, arising as it did in a cultus of asceticism. But we may have another such survival in the character of the Messiah, who associated with publicans and sinners, and in his association with Mary Magdalene, who is portrayed as a former harlot.

The common belief in the early Church that the ministry of Jesus lasted for only one year may also be based on the old usage. Further, as Frazer has suggested, the story of the triumphal entry into Jerusalem may preserve the tradition of a mock-royal procession for the destined victim. The title "Nazarite" may be derived from the word *nazir*, which means dedicated. It is an inheritance from the ancient time when human sacrifice was common and is associated with the myth of Samson in which the shorn Sun-god is, as it were, sacrificed to himself. If so, the Jewish victim, like the Khond, wore his hair unshorn.

We now have enough historic clues to warrant a constructive theory. It frames itself when we collate the data.

1. In the slaying of the Kronian victim at Rhodes, we have an ancient Semitic human sacrifice maintained into the historic period by the expedient of taking as an annual victim a criminal already condemned to death.

2. In Semitic mythology Kronos, "whom the Phoenicians call Israel," sacrifices his son Ieond, "the only," after putting upon him royal robes.

3. The feast of Kronos is the Saturnalia in which elsewhere a mock king plays a prominent part. Kronos was identified among the Semites with Moloch—"King." Hence the victim would be ostensibly either a king or a king's son. A trial and degradation were likely accessories.

4. Supposing the victim in the Rhodian Saturnalia to figure as Ieond, he would be *ipso facto* Barabbas, "the son of the father." At the same time, in terms of the myth he would figure in the royal robes.

5. It is morally certain that among the many cases of human sacrifice in the Graeco-Semitic world the Rhodian rite was not unique. The name Ieond, besides signifying "the only," was virtually identical with the Greek and Hebrew names for Judah (son of "Israel"), and Jew (*Yehuda*, *Iondaios*). The Jews of the Dispersion would be extremely likely to regard it as having special application to their race, which

in their sacred books actually figured as the Only—begotten Son of the Father-God, and as having undergone special suffering.

6. That the Rhodian rite coincided at some points with Jewish conceptions of sacrifice is proved by the detail of leading the prisoner outside the city gates. This is expressly laid down in the Epistle to the Hebrews as a ritual condition of the sacrificed death of Jesus.

The similarity between the Rhodian rite and the story of the crucifixion of Jesus in the Gospels is not exact, but they seem to belong to the same ritual pattern. If the gospel story were real history, this would be a remarkable coincidence. It seems much more probable that the gospel narrative is based on a ritual sacrifice of remote origin of which the Rhodian rite is a variant. The Christian account would therefore be a composite of pre-existing ideas—a myth grown out of ritual. Ideas of a slain and resurrected god, embodied in an annual ritual, are blended with a doctrine of salvation and the institution of a holy sacrament. The religion of Jesus the Christ was founded on this syncretism.

THE MYSTERY PLAY

The manner in which these elements were fused would be by means of a mystery play, as in other religions. In this way the real sacrifice of ancient times passed into a periodic ritual which remained within the fold of Judaism until the fall of Jerusalem. This cult of the Jewish Jesus (Joshua) underwent a change when the Christist movement spread to the Gentile world. The purely Jewish conception of a Messiah was broadened to embrace the Gentiles. The mystery play, not designed to be read but acted, was written in the form of a narrative and was taken to be a record of an historical event.

For the moment we can leave aside the alleged biography and the teaching contained in the gospels. We must turn to the crucifixion story to see whether this description of the sacrifice of a god-man bears the characteristic marks of a dramatic performance, in the light of what we already know of such rituals. The mere possibility that we may be reading the transcript of a play, the basic plot of which is very ancient, meets with instinctive resistance. Yet it is a fact that mystery plays, so far from being uncommon, were a striking feature of the popular religions of Greece and Egypt. There is nothing intrinsically unlikely in the hypothesis that such a drama was in vogue among the Christists.

The sufferings and death of Osiris, for example, were enacted in a sacred drama once a year. Again, Adonis and Attis were represented by effigy in a dramatic ritual. The same is true of Mithra and Dionysus. A performance of the myth of Demeter and Persephone was the central attraction in the Eleusinian mysteries.

There is nothing surprising or unusual in acting out a religious myth. In fact one would expect Christians to imitate paganism and dramatize the Nativity, the Holy Supper, the Crucifixion and the Resurrection. There is a hint of such a drama in the epistle to the Galatians, "before whose eyes Jesus Christ was openly set forth crucified." And again: "I bear in my body the marks of the Lord Jesus." There are other expressions in the epistles describing the devotee as mystically crucified and as having become one with the crucified Lord. They strongly suggest that in the early stages of the cult it dramatically adopted the teaching of the Egyptian Book of the Dead wherein the saved and Osirified soul declares: "I clasp the sycamore tree; I myself am joined into the sycamore tree and its arms are opened unto me graciously." Further, "I have become a divine being by the side of the birthchamber of Osiris; I am brought forth with him, I renew my youth."

The parallels are clear, but we have yet to establish how the drama of Christ's Supper, Passion, Betrayal, Trial and Crucifixion actually *originated*. The proof, I submit, lies before men's eyes in the actual gospel narrative. It has always lain there, but pre-possessions set up by age-long belief have prevented believers and unbelievers alike from seeing it.

Let the reader carefully peruse the series of episodes given in their least sophisticated form in Matthew and Mark. From Matt. xxvi, 17 or 20, the narrative is simply the presentation of a dramatic action and dialogue. The events are huddled one upon the other exactly as happens in all drama that is not framed with a special concern for plausibility. In many plays of Shakespeare and even in the work of Ibsen, the chief master of modern drama—in *Hedda Gabler*, for example—there is a compression of incidents in time to minimize change of scene and develop the action rapidly. To realize fully the theatrical character of the gospel story it is necessary to keep in view this characteristic compression of the action in time, as well as the purely dramatic content. The compression of events not merely proves the narrative to be pure fiction; the reason for the compression is that they are presented in dramatic form.

BETRAYAL AND CRUCIFIXION

As the story stands, Jesus partakes with his disciples of the Passover, an evening meal. After a very brief dialogue they sing a hymn and proceed in the darkness to the Mount of Olives. Nothing is said of what happened or was spoken on the way. The scene is simply changed to the mount; and there a new dialogue and action begin. A slight change of scene—again with no hint of any talk on the way—is made to Gethsemane. The scanty details as to the separation of Jesus from his disciples and the going apart with the three indicate with a brevity obviously dramatic the arrangement by which Judas—who was thus far with the party—would be enabled to withdraw from the stage.

In the Passion scene the dramatic origin of the action is again emphasized. Three times Jesus prays while his disciples are asleep. No one is able to record his words—an incongruity which would not have occurred if the story had been first composed to be read. On the stage, however, there is no difficulty at all since the prayer would be heard by the audience, like a soliliquy. No less striking is the contradiction in verses 45 and 46 where in two successive sentences Jesus tells the sleeping three to sleep on and to arise. What has happened is either a slight disarrangement of the dialogue or the omission of an exit and an entrance.

Then, without the slightest account of what he had been doing in the interim, Judas enters the scene exactly as he would on the stage. With an impossible continuity the action goes on through the night. This would be quite unnecessary save in dramatic fiction where unity of time—Aristotle's limitation of the action within about twenty-four hours—was the ruling principle. Jesus is taken in the darkness to the house of the high priest where the elders were gathered together. The disciples meanwhile had fled. Nothing is said about what they did in the interim, though any account of the epidsode must have come through them if it really happened.

The fact that the whole judicial process took place in the middle of the night shows its unhistorical character. The exigencies of drama are responsible for hunting up "false witnesses" throughout Jerusalem in the dead of night. Jesus is questioned, condemned, buffeted and (presumably) led away; Peter remains on the scene, denies his lord and is convicted of treason by the crowing of the cock. Of what happens to the God-man in the interval there is not a hint, though it is just here that a non-dramatic narrative would follow him most closely.

When morning comes the priests and elders, who have had no rest, take counsel afresh and lead Jesus away to Pilate. This evidently happens off the scene, since we have an interlude in which Judas brings back his thirty pieces of silver, is repudiated by the priests, and goes away to hang himself. The story of the potter's field is obviously an interpolation to explain that "Then was fulfilled that which was spoken by Jeremiah the prophet."

As usual, not a word is said of the details of the transit from place to place. The scene changes all at once to the presence of the Governor and we plunge straight into dialogue. Always we are witnessing drama of which the spectators need no description save when a brief explanation is required of the Barabbas episode. The rest of the trial scene, and the mock-crowning and robing, are strictly dramatic, giving nothing but words and action.

In the account of the trial before Herod, which is found only in Luke, the narrative and non-dramatic form are what we would expect of a later account. The interpolation was doubtless the work of a late Gentile bent on making Jewish and not Roman soldiers guilty of mocking the Lord. Matthew and Mark do not describe the procession to the place of the crucifixion. It is left for Luke to supply the embellishment of the mourning crowd of the daughters of Jerusalem and the speech of Jesus to them on the way.

The Crucifixion and the Resurrection scenes, even the final appearance in Galilee, are set forth in Matthew as they would be represented on a stage. The gospel ends abruptly with the words of the risen Lord. Where the play ended, the narrative ends. Only in the third, later gospel is the story rounded off as a writer who adapted the original play would naturally treat it.

In the non-canonical Gospel of Nicodemus the "Acts of Pilate" have a specifically dramatic form. The material shows that it is later than the canonical gospels. It embodies the water-wine miracle of the mystery play beyond the limits of the first gospel under the pressure of the same Gentile motive. The whole effect is to throw a greater guilt of perversity on the Jews and set Pilate in a favorable light. The resurrection is not directly shown but related by the Roman soldiers. It is as though the compiler was bent on producing new and stronger evidence of its reality.

The "Acts of Pilate" strengthen the presumption of the existence of early dramatic representations of the death of Jesus; it is not to be supposed that the play as it appears in the gospels is in its original form. But if we divide it by its scenes or places we have the classic five acts: (1) the Supper, (2) the Agony and Betrayal on the mount, (3) the trial at the high priest's house, (4) the trial before Pilate, (5) the Crucifixion. If we suppose this to have been one continuous play, the resurrection may have been a separate action with five scenes: (*1*) the removal of the body by Joseph, (*2*) the burial, (*3*) the placing of the guard of soldiers, (*4*) the coming of the women and the address of the angel, (*5*) the appearance of the risen Lord.

The Transfiguration has every appearance of a dramatic representation in the manner of the pagan mysteries. How the scenes may have been originally devised does not affect the essentials of the theory. This is supported by every detail of the structure of the coherent yet impossible story of the Supper, Agony, Betrayal, the two trials, and the Crucifixion. Once this is recognized our conception of the manner of the origin of the gospels is placed on a new, we might say scientific, basis.

PAGAN SAVIORS

In all probability the performance of such a mystery play was suspended in the churches when it had been reduced to narrative form as part of the gospel. This may have occurred either during a time of local persecution or by a deliberate decision in the second century. Such a decision is likely to have been made when the cult, having broken away from Judaism, was also concerned to break away from paganism. What we know of Christian origins suggests that the cult developed in the larger rather than the smaller Hellenistic cities, and it would have needed a fairly strong group to produce such a mystery play. It may indeed never have been performed in full except at such important centers as Antioch or Alexandria. The details of the two Marys suggest Egypt as the possible location of the first performance in its present shape. The cult of Osiris had just such a scene of quasi-maternal mourning. The "lake of fire" and "the second death" in the Apocalypse further point to Alexandrian sources for early Jesuism. But the eucharist, burial and resurrection are Mithraic.

We can only conclude that the death ritual of the Christian creed was framed in a pagan environment and embodies some of the most widespread ideas of pagan religion. The two aspects in which the historic Christ is typically presented to his worshippers, those of his infancy and his death, are typically pagan.

There is not a conception associated with Christ that is not common to some or all of the Savior cults of antiquity. The title Savior was given in Judaism to Yahweh; among the Greeks to Zeus, Helios, Artemis, Dionysus, Heracles, the Dioscuri, Cybele and Aesculapius. It is the essential conception of Osiris. So, too, Osiris taketh away sin, and is judge of the dead, and of the last judgment. Dionysus, Lord of the Underworld and primarily a god of feasting ("the Son of Man cometh eating and drinking"), comes to be conceived as the Soul of the World and the inspirer of chastity and self-purification. From the Mysteries of Dionysus and Isis comes the proclamation of the easy "yoke." Christ not only works the Dionysiac miracle but calls himself "the true vine."

Like Christ, and like Adonis and Attis, Osiris and Dionysus also suffer and die to rise again. To become one with them is the mystical passion of their worshippers. They are all alike in that their mysteries give immortality. From Mithraism Christ takes the symbolic keys of heaven and hell and assumes the function of the virgin-born Saoshyant, the destroyer of the Evil One. Like Mithra, Merodach and the Egyptian Khousu, he is the Mediator; like Khousu, Horus and Merodach, he is one of a trinity; like Horus he is grouped with a divine Mother; like Khousu he is joined with the Logos; and like Merodach he is associated with a Holy Spirit, one of whose symbols is fire.

In fundamentals, therefore, Christism is but paganism reshaped. It is only the economic and the doctrinal evolution of the system—the first determined by Jewish practice and Roman environment, the second by Greek thought—that constitute new phenomena in religious history.

The pagan sources of the eucharist are no less evident. One likely result of ceasing to perform the mystery play would be a modification of the sacramental meal. The constant pagan charge that Christians ate an actual child was met by the Fathers in terms which convey that there was something to conceal. The only satisfactory explanation is that there was an early custom of eating a baked image of a child at Easter communion. Given that the symbol was bread shaped in a human form, Christism was exactly duplicating one of the practices of the Mexicans at the time of the Spanish conquest. But no such primary symbolism was needed when the Christian cult was officially established. The belief that the sacred bread became the flesh of the God, and had miraculous virtue could be maintained on the strength of the bare priestly blessing. The consecrated wafer is itself copied from pagan practice and finally becomes a symbol of a symbol. The tendency in the second and third centuries to use the symbol of a fish, which was employed by the Gnostics, was put down by the Church. The use of the lamb symbol was also discouraged, though it survived with the symbol of the Easter egg which had been taken by the Gnostics from the lore of the Orphicists.

The bread symbol, attenuated to a wafer, gained official acceptance. It preserved the immemorial principle, common to paganism and Judaism, of a constantly repeated sacrifice. The Church of Rome still stands by that doctrine, and the Church of England leans strongly towards it.

It would be helpful now to recapitulate the probable development from dim, primeval times to the rise of Christianity. In the first stage, all victims whether animal or divine are not strictly "sacrificed." They are eaten at the feast which the gods and the dead share. Dead relatives are also eaten and parents filially slain to preserve their qualities in the family or tribe. This would give rise to the sacrifice of human beings at funerals.

Next, these practices would be differentiated into offerings to the gods, totem sacrifices and human sacrifices. Priestly functions would give rise to the conception of ritual sacrifices of animals blessed by the priest and eaten as sacraments, as well as human sacrifices. The latter were progressively modified by substituting a criminal for the king or king's son or first-born.

Thus evolved the idea of a eucharist in which an animal or human being, representing the god, is eaten symbolically or otherwise. When human sacrifices ceased, their place was taken by a mystery drama in which the act of human sacrifice was symbolically represented. The victim is regarded as the unjustly slain god. Inevitably such practices elicited a priesthood. The norm of the priest-administered eucharist is Bread and Wine—Body and Blood. It may, however, take the form of a dough image of an animal, or the God-man or child. The thing eaten may be reduced to a single symbol—e.g. the "communion in one kind" of the Catholic Church which is repudiated by Protestants who revert to "communion in two kinds." The Catholic practice is practically on a par with that of pre-Christian Mexicans; the Protestant reverts to the Mithraic and Dionysiac usages which were imitated by the early Church.

To the uninstructed eye the symbol which results from this long-drawn evolution tells nothing of the dreadful truth, and presents a fable in its place. If to die as a human sacrifice for human beings deserves the highest reverence, the true Christs of the world are to be numbered by millions. Almost every land on the globe has drunk their annually shed blood. Thus has the human race paid in death for its faith in immortality. Nameless men and women have done many millions of times what is credited to the fabulous Jesus of the Christian gospels. They have laid down their lives for the sins of many. Twenty literatures vociferously proclaim the myth, and rivers of tears have been shed at the recital of it, yet the monstrous and inexpugnable truth draws at most a shudder from the student. In a world which still distributes its sympathies in this way, a rational judgment is not to be looked for, save among a few. Delusion as to the course of religious history must long follow in the wake of the delusion which made history possible.

Chapter Five

THE TEACHING-GOD AS LOGOS

Some readers may by now be satisfied that a mystery play on the lines described really existed, but they may feel that this does not entirely dispose of the historicity of Jesus. Critical opinion has become adjusted to the shock that much of the familiar story is mythical. It is prepared to dismiss the account of the virgin birth, the Resurrection and Ascension, together with the miracles. But the point is made that although Jesus never walked on water or turned water into wine, *some* of the things reported of him are entirely credible.

Legends have gathered round many characters whose reality cannot be doubted. May not the same be said about the figure of Jesus? Take away the mythical accretions and we are left, it is said, with a solid core of fact. The sacrificed Savior-god may be a myth derived from a long tradition in which ancient Judaic conceptions either blended with those from pagan sources or underwent a similar evolution. But when the process of syncretism is granted, it is still reasonable to hold that these ideas became attached to a real person whose ethical teaching at least we possess. The myth, in other words, is not sufficient to account for the teaching.

This is the standpoint which is here denied. I am suggesting that there is no reason why we should separate the idea of a Sacrificed-God from that of a teacher subsequently reputed to be divine. Both are myths of a well-known type. Indeed, the formation of secondary Gods regarded as lawgivers and authors of moral codes is part of the normal course of religious evolution. Jesus the Christ is just such a teacher and secondary god.

Although not all secondary gods are sacrificed as saviors, they are nearly always regarded as teachers. Laws and moral precepts are formulated in their name. Some are believed to have brought to their people the boon of new knowledge, such as methods of agriculture. Others have revealed a special wisdom which men could never have acquired by their own efforts. This is true of primitive peoples as well as of more advanced civilizations. Age-old customs and taboos are generally assumed to have had a divine origin.

Among such a primitive tribe as the Narrinyeri of South Australia, the God Nurundere is held to have instituted all the rites and ceremonies. The Babylonian Fish-god, Oannes (or Ea) taught the art of writing, the techniques of agriculture and building, and provided a system of law together with a knowledge of cosmology. The Egyptian Thoth gave men language and names. He taught them writing and the rules of worship and sacrifice. Osiris taught the Egyptians agriculture and laws, just as Janus and Saturn did for the Romans and Huitzilopochtil for the Aztecs. Apollo was also a lawgiver, and he taught the Greeks a more civilized way of life through the oracle at Delphi. Dionysus instructed men in the cultivation of the vine; Demeter introduced agriculture. Isis divides with Osiris the honors of agriculture, having shown men how to make use of wheat and barley.

Goddesses are credited as much as gods with introducing a higher culture. Thus Athene taught all crafts and Cybele, like Isis, is a teacher of healing. The idea of the divine origin of medicine is common to all Aryans. The Gallic Apollo (Grannos or Mabon) and the Teutonic Odin were believed to be able to drive away disease. In Indian mythology also the gods imparted the secrets of healing together with the Veda, or sacred scripture. The same idea is found in Hawaii and Tahiti, and we have already referred to the role attributed to Boora and Tari by the Dravidian Khonds. They raised men from savagery and ignorance to a superior level of existence. Boora exercised a moralizing influence against the cult of human sacrifice.

The Peruvians believed that the Sun had sent Manco Capac and Mama Ocello to teach savage men true religion, morality, agriculture, arts and sciences. According to another myth Pachacamac found the first men so hopeless that he turned them into tiger cats or apes and created a new race to whom he taught arts and handicrafts. This idea of teaching or reformation pervades the whole cosmogony of the Incas. So it was with the Gods of Mexico who were nearly always described as lawgivers. Some invented fire and clothing and at least one was the author of sacred books.

Admittedly there are exceptions in primitive religion. But where the Gods do not teach directly, they do so indirectly by inspiring the priests. In the Tonga Islands the God of artificiers and the arts was served by a priesthood composed of carpenters. When the priest was inspired he spoke in the first person as though for the time being he actually was the God. The divine spirits of deceased nobles also spoke through trance mediumship, and this tended to check the development of the concept of a special teaching God such as we find elsewhere.

Nevertheless, the growth of culture and literature and sacerdotalism favors the emergence of a God who is looked upon as the source of wisdom or revelation. The Assyrian Nabu or Nebo was the embodiment of the wisdom of the Gods as well as being patron of writing and literature. He was the son and interpreter of Merodach, who in turn interpreted the will of his father Ea, an earlier God of wisdom. The Indian Agni had the secondary character of messenger or "Mouth of the Gods." The Egyptian Thoth, originally the Moon-god and "Measurer," becomes the representative of the very principle of instruction and the author of sacred books. In this capacity he gains an advantage over Maat, the Goddess of Law and Truth, who is also both the daughter and mother of Ra. For although every Egyptian God proper is "lord of law" (neb maat), Thoth is in particular the Logos, Reason, or Word, and so becomes the sustainer of Osiris against his enemies.

THE LOGOS CONCEPT

Logos, or the Word, is the Greek form of a concept which appears in many guises from the Mediteranean to China. In its later developments it is part of the terminology of mystical religion and theosophy. It has so many shades of meaning that what it really stands for is difficult to grasp. If we think of Jesus as a mere ethical teacher he seems far removed from the Logos which is referred to in the opening of the fourth gospel: "In the beginning was the Word and Word was with God and the Word was God." We can make nothing of such language if we are ignorant of the strange history of the term. This takes us into a labyrinth of obscure speculation about the function of a secondary God. The word—or teaching—of the God becomes the Word as the personification of the teaching.

In Greek mythology the idea applies in a simple form to Hermes as the Messenger of the Gods. He conveys their will and their teaching. Similarly Apollo is the mouth of Zeus. He reveals the divine counsel through an oracle. Athene, too, is her father's wisdom. But as theosophy developed, Metis becomes the Reason and Intelligence of Zeus personified. The path to a divine teacher is opened up.

The concept of a God as a lawgiver is contained in the myth of Zeus and Minos of Crete. Minosis is a mythical figure who, like Moses, is derived from a deity of an earlier age. It appears again in the legend of Numa and Egeria. The evolution of these concepts has a parallel in development of the principles of law and government in early societies. At first power is vested in the king or tribal chief. As the supreme judge he is a 'God.' In a later stage he is surrounded by a hierarcy of priests, councillors, jurists and administrators and his power is distributed. In effect the Logos is the heavenly Grand Vizier.

We do not know exactly when the Logos-idea reached Judaism. It certainly entered from outside. It could have originated in Greece, Babylon or even India, but Babylon has the best claim. The first known use of the term Logos—as distinct from the idea itself—is by Heraclitus in Ionia, which was within the sphere of Babylonian culture. Max Muller, the eminent Sanskrit scholar, declared that the doctrine is "exclusively Aryan." He wrote that "whoever uses such words as Logos, the Word, *Monogenes*, the Only-begotten, *Prototokos*, the First-Born, *Hyiostou theou*, the Son of God, has borrowed the very germs of his religious thought from Greek philosophy." However, he contradicts this in another passage where he states that the conceptions of the Word as found in the Psalms, and of "the Angel" mentioned in the Pentateuch, are purely Jewish and uninfluenced by Greek thought.

That the Jews derived the idea from India seems even more improbable than that they received it from Greece. But it is plainly present in Indian mythology and is evidently very ancient. The early River-goddess, Sarasvat, becomes identified with Vach (meaning Speech). She appears under different names as the spouse of Brahma and the goddess of wisdom and eloquence, being invoked as the Muse. In the great Indian epic, the Mahabharata, she is called the "mother of the Vedas." The sages are inspired by her.

The conception of the Veda as the Word, the first-created thing, or firstborn Being, is also contained in the Brahamanas. According to Sankara, the Vedantist, "from the eternal Word the world is produced." Again Sabda (the Word) is equated with Brahma (God). But the philosophy of the Logos doctrine is set forth even more explicitly and coherently in China in the sixth century B.C. Lao Tze expounds a doctrine of an all-pervading, primordial Reason (Tao) and a unity and trinity of forms of existence.

The personification of the Word is so old and widespread that it is not obvious where this hypostasis began. It would be far-fetched to suppose that it was transmitted in stages from the Greeks to the Jews and thence to the Persians, the Brahmans and the Chinese. Indeed, the Jews seem to have had the idea before their contact with the Greeks and Mazdeans, and the most reasonable assumption is that in all three cases it came from the same source. The religion of Babylon contains the principle of the Logos in its most definite primary form. The concept of the Divine Name had much of the mystic significance of Logos, which meant both "word" and "reason." This developed into the personification of divine Wisdom as an entity—a secondary God—dwelling beside the deity. This was the germ of Plato's doctrine of Ideas no less than of Johannine theology and the mysticism of Philo. The most reasonable assumption is that the concept first emerged from the vast accumulation of fancies and speculations in the lore of the Babylonians. It may have been present in the ancient civilization from which that of China itself was derived.

Further evidence for a central source is found in the doctrine common to Indian, Greek and Babylonian systems that all things originate from a watery abyss, and again from the cosmic egg. Indian lore combines the idea of creation through water and through the word in the double-meaning of *saras*, which can be taken as Water and Voice—hence Sarasvati is not only "the watery" but "the vocal." Agni, the Fire-god, who is finally identified with the Word, is described as the Son of Water and the messenger of the Gods. And the Babylonian Ea, the Water-god and Lord of Life, is also father of the Fire-god who is messenger and counsellor of the Gods. The characteristics of Sarasvati are found in the Baylonian goddess Sarpanitum who, as finally blended with Erua, the daughter of Ea, is at once "lady of the deep," "voice of the deep," and "the possessor of knowledge concealed from men."

Behind the confusion of these various attributes—which is due to their gradual evolution—we can discern the close association in the Babylonian mind of wisdom and the life-giving principle and water. Here, surely, in this complex of myths and ideas, we have the germs of the Hindu. Heraclitean and Platonic concepts of the Word or Reason; of Hermes as Logos and Messenger of the Gods; of Apollo as his father's wisdom; of the Hindu, the Hebrew and the Greek formulas of the Firstborn and Only-begotten; and so, too, of the later Jewish and Christian theosophy. The more we study the cults and creeds of Asia Minor and Syria, the more clearly we see their relation to the great mass of Babylonian theosophy which was still a culture force in the earlier centuries of the Christian era. It gave to the Christian Gnostics their astrology and magic, their doctrine of the immortality of souls (not bodies), their Sophia and conception of a Savior, Knowledge-giver and Mediator. It is a rational presumption that it gave the concept of the Logos to Greek and Jew alike.

JEWISH SPECULATIONS

The Jews, then, received the idea of the Logos from speculations already in existence, and it grew in a piecemeal fashion.

Affinities with more primitive thought are suggested by the beliefs in our own day of the Yorubas of Nigeria who probably also owed them to Semitic or eastern sources. Their general concept of the Mother of All behind that of a natural trinity of Father, Mother and Son, tended to be superseded by a male God, perhaps with the decline of matriarchy. Some such progression seems also to have taken place among the Hebrews. The original feminine "Holy Spirit" had been kept very much in the background, perhaps in fear of contamination by a Goddess worship which symbolized sexuality and fecundity by the dove. For the later Christists, the dove represented its opposite —chastity.

But the myth-making faculty was stronger than dogma and stronger than fear. Accordingly we have Philo, at the beginning of the Christian era, accumulating round the Logos the various aspects of the earlier Word and Sophia. By adding to them the notions of Sonship and Messiahship, and even the creative function of Demiourgos, he at times reduced Yahweh to a somewhat remote abstraction.

It was long supposed that Philo must have borrowed his ideas from the Christians. There can be no question that they are paralleled by Christian doctrines, especially the fourth gospel. They may even have been tampered with. But if so, it was not by Christian hands. The Christian frauds, such as the Sibylline predictions, betray themselves at a glance, whereas no passages in Philo have that hallmark.

What, then, did Philo teach? An examination of his many references to the Logos reveals a maze of inconsistencies. The Logos is variously described as a deity, a spoken utterance, a creative power, the firstborn son of the deity, a high priest and mediator, the covenant, the corrdinating law of the universe, an eternal entity, the first created thing, the chief of angels, the sun, the Scriptures, Moses, an abstraction of wisdom, the soul of the world. But language like this belonged to the mental climate of the age. Clarity and consistency were impossible. Philosophic thought was a shapeless cloud of words and verbal images. Simpler people reduced all these vague abstractions to personalities without qualification.

In the Book of Enoch, long before Philo, the Messiah is identified with a First-Created power with the characteristics of the Logos. For most neologising Jews, the Logos was a person. They could not help thinking in this way. The perpetual naming of an abstraction in religious lore or ritual sets up for the believer an idea of separate personality, or nothing. Their ancestors had personified winds, rivers, diseases, thunder and lightning. Philo, in spite of his superior resources, does not break with this animistic way of thinking. If the mind of a modern scholar cannot express the Logos idea without contradiction, still less could an Alexandrian Jew. The conclusion is clear: the Christian doctrine of the Logos is a dogmatic deposit, round the nucleus of a sacramental cult of the vaporous haze of thought set up in the Jewish world by Yahwistic speculation on Gentile notions.

It was the presence of the Jesuist nucleus that wrought the solidification. Philo himself was too occupied with allegory and symbol and abstraction to give the Logos dogmatic definition. He saw no bar to the multiplication of Logoi. Besides treating Moses and Aaron as Logoi, he has a multitude of lesser Logoi who figure endlessly as thoughts, words, angels, laws, forces and reasons. There is nothing to show that he ever asked himself what he understood by personality. Jesuism was responsible for excluding further vacillation by precipitating the Logos-Idea on the eucharistic sacrifice. The concept of the Sophia was no less potentially adaptable, but it only came to birth in Gnostic teachings and was finally suppressed by the Church.

Philo's doctrine of the Holy Spirit, on the other hand, found acceptance in the formula of the Christian Trinity. The male Spirit has always remained an extremely dim conception, and there are many grounds for regarding the female Sophia as more suitable. She would have supplied the normal demand for a Mother-goddess. But asceticism was in the ascendant when the doctrine of the Trinity was formulated. This vetoed the admission of a goddess. The craving for a Teaching-god was satisfied by identifying the Sacrificed-god with the Logos. It would have been equally natural—but for the temporary dominance of the ascetic principle—to identify Mary with both Sophia and the Spirit (originally feminine). As it was, the exaltation of Mary came about afterwards as a result of stressing the metaphysical aspects of the Son. It was then too late to graft a dogmatic

Sophia on the new sacred books. An attempt at a new gospel in the thirteenth century was crushed by the preponderating power of the Papacy. But it is none the less clear that the doctrine of the Logos is a product of the same process of primitive psychology as produces deities of any order.

Chapter Six

THE QUEST FOR THE HISTORICAL JESUS

Although the personified Word fulfils some of the requirements of a Teaching-god, it is much too abstract for most people to grasp. There is a gulf between the figure of Jesus who went about preaching and attracting followers and this abstruse, theological conception. Indeed, when we try to reconcile the fourth gospel with the synoptics, the Logos is a stumbling block. For centuries men have revered and loved the figure of Jesus that they have extracted from the gospel accounts. The enormous volume of pious literature that has accumulated obscures the contradictions which have puzzled scholars. The latter have made elaborate and ingenious attempts to explain the discrepancies away. It is only in comparatively modern times that the possibility was considered that Jesus does not belong to history at all. Those who come across this idea for the first time are naturally startled by it. In fact the suspicion that Jesus might be as mythical as such ancient saviors as Osiris, Mithra and Krishna arose as a result of a serious effort to discover his real voice and actions. The most scrupulous analysis of the texts failed to reveal a convincing picture of an authentic person.

Modern biblical critics freely admit that some of the gospel narrative must be fiction. We know now that it was composed well after the events it purports to describe. Comparative religion has drawn attention to close pagan parallels—to the essential features of the story—the virgin birth, the sacrificial death and resurrection. The same is true of the rites of baptism and sacramental communion. Many critics still feel, however, that these are accretions which, together with the miracles, can be safely shed without injury to a nucleus of historical fact. They argue that although pagan gods may have some of the attributes of Jesus, and although they may have been regarded as lawgivers and teachers, they did not leave behind a coherent and profound teaching. Apollo, Osiris and the rest seem, therefore, to be obviously mythical, whereas Buddha and Jesus are not. The teachings of each of the latter, it is felt, bear the unmistakeable stamp of a single, unique mind. Such a doctrine could not have formed itself spontaneously.

We shall consider the case of Buddha later. First let us look at the main objections to this view that the existence of a body of teaching is overwhelming evidence of the existence of an historical teacher. The earliest Christian documents are those ascribed to Paul. These epistles were written long before the canonical gospels were put together and accepted by the Church. The older portions, however, tell us nothing about the life of Jesus. The silence of Paul is remarkable if he was indeed familiar with the Jesuine biography. Secondly, the unity of teaching which, it is said, would show it to have been the work of one mind, is conspicuously absent. So far from displaying coherence, the ethical precepts are frequently obscure and contradictory. So far from being original, many of the sayings are merely quotations from earlier Hebrew literature, and some have pagan parallels. As for the Sermon on the Mount, of which so much is made, it is no more than a patchwork of utterances found in the Old Testament.

For over a hundred years German scholars have been struggling to solve this problem, and their efforts have been unavailing. In order to establish some solid textual foundation for the historicity of Jesus, they have piled hypothesis on hypothesis with ever new refinements. The retreat from this hopeless task was finally sounded by the eminent German critic, O. Schmiedel. After an exhaustive search, he was satisfied that he had discovered some texts which passed the most severe tests and were entirely credible. But in the whole of the gospels all he could salvage were *nine* such texts. Let us enumerate this forlorn handful of unwounded survivors.

1) Mark XXX. 17 f.f. "Why callest thou me good?", etc.
2) Matt. XII. 31 f.f.Blasphemy against the Son of Man pardonable
3) Mark III.21 "He is beside himself"
4) Mark XII.32 "Of that day and hour knoweth no man," etc.
5) Mark XV.34. Matt. XXvii.46 "My God, my God, why hast thou forsaken me?"
6) Mark VIII.12 "No sign shall be given to this generation"
7) Mark VI.5 "He was able to do no mighty work"
8) Mark viii.14–21 Rebuke to disciples concerning bread and leaven.
9) Matt.XI.5. Luke VII.22 Passage to be taken in the sense of *spiritual* healing, since it ends with mention of preaching—not a miracle at all.

Why select these particular texts and no others? Schmiedel proceeds on the following principle: where Jesus speaks simply as a man, making no pretense to divinity, or to miraculous powers, and where he is represented as failing to impress his relatives and neighbors with any sense of his superiority—there the record is entirely credible. According to Schmiedel, these passages represent "the foundation pillars for a truly scientific life of Jesus. . . . They prove not only that in the person of Jesus we have to do with a completely human being, and that the divine is to be sought in him only in the form in which it is capable of being found in a man; *they also prove that he really did exist*, and that the Gospels contain at least *some absolutely trustworthy facts* concerning him."

This will shock the believer without satisfying the scientific naturalist. I submit that the proposition I have italicized is absolutely untenable. On this point may be staked the whole dispute about the actuality of the gospel Jesus. It simply does not follow that because a statement is credible it is therefore trustworthy or proved. If it were so, half the characters in fiction could be "proved" to be real people. Perfectly credible statements are made about them.

What applies to characters in fiction must also apply to demigods and characters about whom there is a fable. Unless it can be shown on independent grounds how the credible story came to be associated with the fable, we have no reason to accept the one and reject the other. There are many instances of myths being built up on a basis of actual events, but although this can be established in modern times, such cases do not enable us to distinguish between the merely possible and the true in ancient tradition. Admittedly there are borderline cases, but even when these are free from supernaturalism they may often be doubted. The task of the historian is to make a rational selection.

The historian must avoid the type of illicit leap made, for example, by T. H. Huxley, who was very accommodating in his attitude to what is "possible." With regard to the story of Saul's visit to the witch of Endor, for example, he observed that "it does not matter very much whether the story is historically true, it is quite consistent with probability." He then goes on to say that he sees no reason to doubt that Saul made such a visit. But unless we can show that the story was reduced to writing near the time of Saul, there is certainly a reason to doubt it. History is full of discredited "probabilities" of the same kind. The story of Bruce and the spider is a further example.

To return to Schmiedel's argument for the historicity of Jesus, it can be stated briefly as follows: the gospels ascribe hundreds of unlikely sayings to Jesus, but there are nine which are likely. The nine not only establish that Jesus existed, but they also give some basis for the opinion that many of the less likely are historical. On this reasoning, if only ten reasonable sayings, as well as twelve more or less unlikely labors, had been ascribed to Heracles, he could be considered an historical character.

The fact is that the gospel Jesus won belief much more in virtue of the hundreds of improbabilities and falsities than on the strength of the "credible" texts. That being so, there is no reason to surmise a nucleus of actuality which was never demanded. We would expect to find a certain number of plausible sayings in any fictitious narrative. The willingness to believe the implausible statement can be explained by the desire of certain men or sects to give the authority of the God-man to their views. What, then, does it signify that a few relatively reasonable sayings were attributed to Jesus? What plausibility remains of the cry on the Cross, "My God, why hast thou forsaken me?" when we remember that it is a quotation from the Psalms, and that the whole cult proceeded from the doctrine that "the Christ must needs suffer"?

THE SILENCE OF PAUL

It may seem ungracious to press the argument against a theologian who has gone further in his loyalty to the critical principle than many professed rationalists. What he and others do not recognize, however, is that the primary reason for doubting the genuineness of every detail of teaching in the gospels is the total ignorance of those teachings shown in the Pauline epistles. Allowing for the fact that some are spurious and others contain interpolations, their importance is that they are ostensibly the oldest documents of the Christian cult. Yet they show little awareness of the teaching and narrative of the gospels. They speak of a crucified Jesus in terms of a slain and resurrected God, or demi-god, rather than of the teacher and wonder-worker of the gospels.

The only saying of Jesus actually quoted concerns the origin of the Eucharist (1 Cor: XI, 23–25), and this bears the mark of interpolation. The general tenor of the Epistles—whatever their date or ownership—is incompatible with the development described in the gospels. Higher criticism of the New Testament has missed the way, just as higher criticism of the Old did by taking for granted the general truth of tradition. The Book of Judges, for example, describes a state of Hebrew society which is incompatible with what was supposed to have preceded it. The traditional story of the Exodus and the tabernacle of the desert must therefore be mythical. Similarly, the Christian tradition of a preaching and cult-founding Jesus is accepted by higher critics, although an intelligent perusal of the Pauline epistles suffices to show that the preaching Jesus was created after they were written.

The Jesus of the Pauline doctrine was either a mythical construction or a remote figure thought to have been crucified but no longer traceable in history. A Jesus ben Pandira is said to have been stoned and hung on a tree under the Hasmonean King,

Alexander Jannaeus, nearly a hundred years before the Christian era. It is conceivable that Paul's Jesus is merely a nominal memory of the slain Jesus ben Pandira. In that case, Paul himself may belong to an earlier period than tradition assigns to him. The most genuine looking epistles in themselves give no decisive clue as to chronology. But such a shifting of Paul's date would not help the case for "Jesus of Nazareth." If the difficulty of Paul's silence is avoided by placing him a generation or more earlier, we are faced by the fresh incredibility of a second crucified Jesus, a second sacrificed Son of God, vouched for by records which are mostly false, although they contain a fraction of plausible narrative.

When we turn from the reputed teaching of Jesus to the story of his career, the presumption that it has a factual basis is so slender as to be negligible. The Church found it so difficult to settle the date of its alleged founder's birth that the Christian era was made to begin some years before the year which chronologists later inferred on the strength of other documents. The nativity was placed at the winter solstice, thus coinciding with the birthday of the Sun-god. And the date of the crucifixion was made to vary from year to year to conform to the astronomical principle which fixed the Jewish Passover. In between the birth and death of Jesus, there is an almost total absence of information except about the brief period of his ministry. Of his life between the ages of twelve and thirty we know nothing. There are not even any myths. It is impossible to establish with accuracy the duration of the ministry from the gospels. According to tradition it lasted one year, which suggests that it was either based on the formula "the acceptable year of the Lord," or on the myth of the Sun-god.

The Christian myth grew by absorbing details from pagan cults. The birth story is similar to many nativity myths in the pagan world. The Christ had to have a virgin for a mother. Like the image of the child-god in the cult of Dionysus, he was pictured in swaddling clothes in a basket manger. He was born in a stable like Horus—the stable-temple of the virgin goddess Isis, queen of heaven. Again like Dionysus, he turned water into wine; like Aesculapius, he raised men from the dead and gave sight to the blind; and like Attis and Adonis, he is mourned and rejoiced over by women. His resurrection took place, like that of Mithra, from a rock-tomb.

Since Jesus was a Jewish Savior before the spread of the cult led to a Gentile Christ, the myth had also to satisfy Messianic ideas. Jewish tradition expected a Messiah Ben-David and a Messiah Ben-Joseph, and so Jesus was made to descend from David by a royal line and to become Ben-Joseph through his putative father. To satisfy those who denied the need for a descent from David, the story that Jesus repudiated the claim was inserted in the gospels, and the discrepancy was allowed to remain. The massacre of the innocents at his birth recalls the Moses myth. As in the sacrifice of "the only begotten Son" of the Semitic God El, and the sacrificed God-man of the Babylonian feast of Sacaea, Jesus had to bear the insignia of royalty at his crucifixion.

What might seem at first to be a real biography is dwarfed by this mythical framework. Above all, as we have already seen, the central event of the crucifixion as depicted in the gospels was written up from a mystery play. This can be accounted for as a development, like the pagan mystery dramas, from a primitive rite of human sacrifice to which the very name "Jesus" probably belonged. The gospel version could have been adapted from an earlier, Judaic form by Gentile Christists after the fall of Jerusalem.

JEWISH JESUISM

On this view the Christist movement was originally a Jewish sect. The existence of Jewish and Gentile strands, sometimes resisting fusion, is clear from the disputes and contradictions that developed. The early Jesuists felt themselves as belonging to the Jewish fold and believed that the Messiah would soon return in power and glory on the Day of Judgment. Against this is the rival conception of the kingdom of heaven as a purely spiritual change. In one gospel Samaritans and Gentiles are excluded; and in another Samaritans are extolled. The ethical teaching is both particularist and universalist. It demands the uttermost fulfilment of Mosaic law and yet claims to supersede it.

There was hardly anything in the Christian system incompatible with Jewish thought. The Hebrew scriptures speak just as sympathetically of the poor. Although the narrow traditionalism ascribed to the Pharisees is condemned, it may be contrasted with the liberal views of such rabbis as Hillel. "The law of the heart" was certainly no invention of the Christists.

Early Jesuism flourished as a means of Jewish proselytism, but in order to spread, it had to come to terms with those features which the Gentiles resented. There was the clash over ritual food requirements, and most of all over circumcision. And there was the practical problem of the financial demands of the Jewish hierarchy which made the temple of Jerusalem the fiscal headquarters of the faithful. The early Jesuists expected Gentile converts to contribute to the central funds in the same way as Orthodox Jews, dispersed throughout the empire, paid tribute to travelling "collectors" who followed them up. As the movement took root in the Gentile world this centralization was resisted.

We must not suppose that Jewish Jesuism arose primarily as a moral revolt against the legalistic ethics stigmatized as "Pharasaism." Its ethics were neither superior to nor different from those already contained in the Hebrew tradition. In any case a mass movement requires more than high ethical ideals in order to succeed. Unless the appeal aimed first at the Jews could be broadened by directing it to proselytes and then to Gentiles, it would have made no striking progress.

The substitution of baptism for circumcision was one concession. The admission of slaves to full membership was another. The subsequent establishment of self-supporting communities of believers encouraged more than financial independence. Despite opposition from Jerusalem the movement was bound to become more cosmopolitan. Its propaganda was adapted accordingly, special emphasis being laid in the Gentile passion-play, on the guilt of the Jews for the rejection of the Savior.

The upshot of this breakaway of the Gentile Christists from the Jewish Jesuists was the emergence of a new sect which was able to compete with the numerous mystery religions already existing in the Graeco-Roman world. Freed from the control of the Jerusalem community, the Gentile Christists were able to adapt themselves to the needs of the time. Inevitably this exposed their increasingly pagan influences. The whole conception of a purely spiritual, as distinct from temporal, salvation which grew up in the Gentile churches is Hellenistic or Persian rather than Jewish. So is the title "Savior," and the idea that those who partake of a mystic rite become one with the crucified demi-god. We are driven to the conclusion that the central figure of the cult represented in the gospels must be a construction of propagandists rather than a biography. The Christ so depicted has no more claim to be historical than the other Saviors and divine teachers of antiquity. None of the pagan teachers worshipped as a god is derived from a real teacher or lawgiver, and the same can be said of such revered founders of codes and creeds as Manu, Lycurgus, Numa and Moses. Even scholars who still speak of Moses as an historical person must concede that he wrote nothing. He can no more be supposed to have invented the Ten Commandments than Romulus or Numa the Twelve Tables.

Claims have been made for the historicity of Zarathustra, but they cannot be proved by any documentary evidence. The only reason for believing that he was a real person is the presumption that this is always how a religious movement originates. But whenever the tradition tells of a founder of doctrines or mysteries, a critical search finds myth. If we take the whole series of traditional teachers down to the Christian era, we find them to be more or less clearly the products of the same tendency which led to the conception of a series of Teaching-gods—the habit of supposing that everything held to be good must have come from a divine or supernormal source.

MYTH AND HISTORY

One objection that may be raised at this point is that some religious founders have unquestionably been real persons. What a man has admittedly done, it may be argued, may well have been done in more ancient times by other men. If Mohammed founded a new religion, why not Zoroaster? If Buddha gave a virtually new and potent teaching, why may not Jesus have done so?

Let us consider first why we accept the historicity of Mohammed. (1) He is far down within the historic period. (2) His religion rose to power and notoriety within a generation of his death—a far swifter development than that of Christism, although its spread is so often described as miraculous. (3) He actually left written documents, and although they were certainly edited, most of them are free from the well-known marks of late fabrication. (4) In virtue of the relation of Islam to Christianity, which claimed a monopoly of truth for its sacred books, a critical light played upon the new cult from the first days of its expansion beyond Arabia. (5) The biographical accounts of Mohammed are not typically mythical, apart from tales of marvels at his birth and infancy. Apart from such embellishments, and references to intercourse with angels, Mohammed is born and lives and dies at known dates. He works no miracles and makes no claim to divinity. He is, in short, recognizable as an historic type of masterful fanatic. In every one of these respects his record differentiates sharply from that of Buddha and Jesus.

Absolute date, of course, is not a decisive consideration. We believe in the historicity of certain Jews B.C., and we disbelieve in the legend of William Tell. But when we consider the environments in which Jesus and Buddha are supposed to have lived, it is clear that the possibilities of fable growing round such names are boundless. Neither Jesus nor Buddha left a written word; nor do critical scholars claim that their immediate associates did so. It is admitted that many sayings are falsely ascribed to both. Instead of letting the supposed historicity of Buddha plead for that of Jesus, we are led to ask whether the one is not as problematic as the other.

As soon as we start to investigate Buddhist origins we become aware of a dilemma. It would seem that although the Buddha did not directly repudiate the belief in deities, he ignored it as valueless. The movement which was set up in his name was practically atheistic. On the other hand, the legends of his birth and life are in terms of supernaturalistic beliefs of earlier and later times.

The conservative student naturally answers that though a perversion of the Master's teaching did take place, he remains nonetheless a real person. The usual proof offered is that the many narratives represent him speaking like any other mortal teacher. However, a close scrutiny shows that every cause of scepticism that exists in the case of Jesus and Moses is also present here, with differences only of degree. There are no contemporary records, and many of the subsequent versions of Buddha's teaching are plainly untrustworthy. Much of the teaching put in his mouth is of a nature known to have been current before his period.

The teaching not only contains the sort of inconsistencies which are perhaps inevitable, but we soon notice differences of source, time and aim. It is hard to conceive how such a metaphysical doctrine could have inspired a far-reaching popular movement, or why it should have given rise to any religious society whatever. Yet when we turn to the earliest Buddhist literature, we find all the marks of doctrinal myth. The books of the Sutta Pitaka, for example, not only profess to contain the belief itself, but the belief as the Buddha uttered it. For the Buddhist community it was indissolubly bound up with the memory of the personality of him who had proclaimed it. We are told that after the Dhamma, or collection of short scriptures, was promulgated, a desire sprang up to know how Buddha himself came to lay down the Rule to his disciples.

Here, then, we have yet another instance of a cult creating its Teaching-god on familiar lines, describing him as supernaturally born, calling him the Blessed One, visibly inventing for the traditional teacher a fictitious biography. At this early stage Buddhism is seen making its Buddha. So far from providing an analogy to support the historicity of Jesus, it does the reverse. It vividly suggests that a similar process of construction occurred in the case of Christism. We are left merely asking what primitive Buddhism really was.

Chapter Seven

THE BUDDHA MYTH

According to tradition, the founder of Buddhism was a Hindu named Siddhattha, son of the rajah of the Sakyan clan which dwelt in the foothills of the Himalayas. He is sometimes referred to as Sakyamuni (*muni* meaning Sage), sometimes as Tathagata (literally "One who has come, or gone, This Far"), more usually as Gotama Buddha. The term Buddha is a title, not a personal name. Gotama is referred to as the Buddha after his Enlightenment, which is reputed to have occurred in 528 B.C. in Bihar. Thereafter he abandoned family life and promulgated his doctrine of deliverance from suffering and the attainment of ultimate peace, Nirvana.

His teaching is called the Dhamma (Sanskrit Dharma), and is summed up in the Four Noble Truths and the Noble Eightfold Path. The essentials are too well known to be stated here in detail. Briefly, it holds that life is bound up inevitably with suffering. We crave for happiness either in this or some future life, and until we end desire and become non-attached, suffering is inescapable. The eightfold Way of Life is a middle path which avoids ascetic extremes. It consists of Right Views, Right Mindedness, Right Speech, Right Action, Right Livelihood, Right Endeavor, Right Mindfulness and Right Concentration. Salvation is liberation from the chain of rebirth. It is achieved solely by our own efforts.

There were many sects and sages in India 2500 years ago, but their teachings were transmitted orally. The Buddhist Dhamma was not written down for centuries after it had been first enunciated. The various Sanskrit and Pali texts which purport to contain the original teaching are therefore the product of evolution, and it is impossible to say which of the divergent interpretations, if any, represents the pristine form. What is quite certain is that the underlying philosophy had a great deal in common with ideas prevalent at the time. It bears some resemblance to the contemporary Jainist movement.

The breakaway from Hindu ritualism was not a unique innovation; neither was there anything new in the founding of an order of monks. Various sects were already organized as mendicant monks, and it was an established custom for them to meet periodically and proclaim their teaching in public. The early Buddhists followed this familiar pattern. They made modifications, of course, and one feature was the rejection of the severe austerities which were practiced by some of the sects.

THE SERIES OF BUDDHA

Not only have we no sixth-century record of the rules of the Buddhist Sangha, as the order was called, but it did not claim to be a new teaching. The tradition holds that it had been promulgated many times before—that Gotama was only one of a long series of Buddhas who arise at intervals and who all teach the same doctrine. The names of twenty-four of such Buddhas who appeared before Gotama have been recorded. The number and names may well be late inventions, but there can be no question about the belief in their existence. It was held that after the death of each Buddha, his religion flourishes for a time and then decays. After it is forgotten, a new Buddha emerges and preaches the lost Dhamma, or Truth. In the fourth century A.D. a sect of Buddhists rejected Gotama and venerated instead the three previous Buddhas. They especially reverenced one of them, Kasyapa, and were actually joined by the orthodox in worship at his tomb.

It seems quite probable in the light of these facts that any number of teachings attributed to "the Buddha" may have been in existence either before or at the time when Gotama was believed to have lived. They might all have been attributed to a sage with the title of "the Blessed One." They might include teachings that were ascribed later to Gotama.

The name Gotama is a common one; it is also full of mythological associations. There was admittedly *another* Gotama known to the early Buddhists, who founded an order. So what proof is there that the sayings and doings of different Gotamas may not have been ascribed to one person? Again, assuming that the Four Noble Truths and the Noble Eightfold Path are the oldest doctrines of the Buddhist movement, and were formulated by one Gotama, what reason is there to believe that the movement either arose or made progress on the simple basis of his teachings?

Baur, while believing in the historicity of Jesus, nevertheless avows: "How soon would everything true and important that was taught by Christianity have been relegated to the series of long-faded sayings of the noble humanitarians and thinking sages of antiquity, had not its teachings become words of eternal life in the mouth of its Founder?" Similarly, may we not ask, how, in much-believing India, could any large organized movement develop on the simple nucleus of a teaching of self-control, which differed from the common practice of Hindu asceticism only in its renunciation of positive self-maceration? Supposing a sage to have framed an eightfold path including Right Means of Livelihood, how should he intelligibly proceed to establish his way by forming an Order of *Mendicants*? It may be argued that he was giving a preference to mendicancy over the *wrong* means such as fortune-telling and astrology, which were practiced by some recluses and Brahmins, but on this view "rightness" is merely negative.

THE DOCUMENTARY EVIDENCE

No doubt one answer will be that the above is an *a priori* objection and that we must take the evidence as we find it in the oldest documents. In the books of the Pali canon the teaching is passed on in collections of *suttas*—a word which means "thread." When these are examined, however, they fail to yield reliable information on important points. Thus the Mahapurinibhana-Sutta gives an account of the heresy which the First Buddhist Council was summoned to deal with, but the author has no knowledge of the First Council. Moreover, Buddha is represented as saying that unless a certain tribe—the Vaggians—honor and support shrines in their country, and allow the proper rites to be performed, their prosperity will decline. But this sharply conflicts with the opposition to prayers and sacrifices which is held to be characteristic of Buddhism as a reformist movement.

Pali scholars are more and more convinced that the First Council is a literary myth. There is scepticism also about the tradition that a Second Council was held at Vesali a hundred years after Buddha's death. It may have been centuries later. Its object was to agree upon uniformity of rules of discipline and procedure in the Sangha. But the Vinaya texts, which contain such rules, have nothing of the nature of innovating propaganda. They entirely lack the sort of appeal that would create a new Order. Rather, they correspond to the late code of monastic rules framed for monastic orders in Christendom. The fact that they are all ascribed to the Founder is one more evidence of the total lack of critical historical sense among the members.

Looking, then, for a foothold among the shifting sands of Buddhist tradition we note the following clashing records:

(1) The Buddha is represented in ostensibly early and late tradition as speaking of the Gods with full belief in their existence.

(2) He is represented on the one hand as discouraging sacrifices, and on the other as prescribing for a whole tribe a strict adherence to ancient rites.

(3) King Asoka, who figured as a good Buddhist in the early vigor of the movement, about 250 B.C., habitually called himself "the delight of the Gods" as did his contemporary, "the pious Buddhist king of Ceylon."

(4) The Buddha is represented as throwing his Order open to all classes and at the same time making the name "Brahmin" a term of honor for his Arahats or saints. Brahmins were among his most distinguished disciples.

(5) On the principle that Buddha delivered the whole canon, much teaching that certainly did not come from him is ascribed to him.

(6) Much of the philosophy set forth as his teaching is identical

with the Sankhya system, germs of which are admittedly pre-Buddhistic.

What doctrines, it must now be asked, were special to Buddhism? Not Karma, that was common property which Buddhism shared. Not in asserting that a right mind was superior to sacrifice, that was a primary doctrine of the Jains, and pre-Buddhistic, both within and without the pale of Brahmanism. Not in seeking a way of salvation independently of the Vedas, that had been done by many teachers in various sects. Not in the doctrine that defilement comes not from unclean meats but from evil deeds and words and thoughts; Buddhist writers themselves say that it is derived from previous Buddhas. Not in the search for peace through self-control and renunciation; that was the quest of a myriad recluses and all previous Buddhas. Not in the view that there is a higher wisdom than that attained by austerities; that, too, is pre-Buddhistic. Not in the doctrine that non-Brahmans could join an Order and attain religious blessedness; other orders were open to men of low social status and even to slaves. Indeed, the rigid separation of caste was not yet established in the early days of Buddhism. Brahmin claims were exorbitantly high, but many Brahmins waived them and they did not apply to ascetics. Early Buddhists, like the early Christians, did not admit runaway slaves to the Order.

The admission of women was not an innovation as it was practiced by the Jains, and even the tradition makes the Buddha accept it reluctantly in the twenty-fifth year of his preaching. There seems, in short, to be nothing on the face of the doctrine to account for the expansion of the Buddhist movement. We are therefore led to search for possible sociological explanations.

HOW BUDDHISM SPREAD

The reasons why so many people joined the Buddhist Order is examined in the *Milinda Prashnaya*. A number of questions are put by Milinda—who has been identified with the Greek king Menander of Sagala, in the Punjab, c.150 B.C.—to Nagasena, the founder of a northern school of Buddhism. Milinda asks whether all members join for the high end of renunciation. "Certainly not, sire," replies Nagasena. "Some for these reasons, but some have left the world in terror at the tyranny of kings. Some have joined us to be safe from being robbed; some harassed by debt; and some perhaps to gain a livelihood."

This gives some idea of the social conditions, but the same pressures would drive men to join other Orders. We have still to ask why Buddhism was such a powerful attraction.

To begin with, there are strong reasons for thinking that the Jains and Buddhists were originally either simple sects or parts of one sect of Brahmanism. The latter is believed by some scholars to have split on two main lines, the one finding the First Cause in matter, the other in spirit. The spirit theory gradually become an orthodoxy; the alternative, heterodox view led to more practical questions and became the basis of Buddhism. Thus in Weber's *History of Indian Literature*, the quasi-atheistic element in Buddhism is seen as primordial, and the Jains are regarded as only one of the earliest Buddhist sects. The Buddha proclaimed nothing new. He merely made public what had been believed by a few anchorites.

Other authorities diverge to the extent of holding that the Jains and the Buddhists were independent sects from the beginning. The fact that the Buddhists opposed the Brahmanic doctrine of Atman, or personal soul, whereas the Jains accepted it with modifications and taught that animals and plants had souls, supports the view that they had always been separate. But there is a significant affinity in the legends of the two sects. Mahavira, the great hero of the Jains, preached in the same district as Buddha, and is actually described as the son of Siddhattha—the personal name of Gotama. The legends of both are interwoven with the history of Krishna.

Whatever may be the truth of their relationship in this obscure period, Buddhism does not emerge clearly as an established system until it was adopted by King Asoka, about 250 B.C. His edicts show that only a small number of scriptures were then recognized as the spoken discourses of the Buddha. Among those named is "The Terrors of the Future" which describes the different worlds of purgatory. So that even at this early date in the known history of the Order, a doctrine is attributed to Buddha which he elsewhere is supposed to have repudiated.

The success of Buddhism cannot be explained by the novelty

of its ideas since many of them already existed. And if ideas alone do not supply the answer, we must consider what part was played by social forces. There must have been some other reason than doctrine which made Asoka and the King of Ceylon favor the Buddhist order. We know that Constantine made Christianity the state religion because of its obvious political uses as a far-reaching organization. Had the Kings of Magadha a similar motive?

A robber chief named Chandragupta seized the throne of Magadha, murdering the rajah, about 315 B.C. He defeated the Greek governor of the Indus provinces and drove Greek power out of India. At that time the Buddhists appeared to be a party of reform, making light of caste distinctions. Their support would naturally be welcomed by the usurper and his low caste followers from the Punjab, especially as the influence of the Brahmins must have been exerted against them. In any case, the peoples of the Punjab had retained their ancient Vedic standpoint, free and independent, without either priestly domination or a caste system. If Chandragupta and his Punjabis accepted Buddhism, they would be strengthening the tendency to ignore caste. Magadha was a border province, never completely Brahmanized so the native inhabitants might have welcomed this opportunity to rid themselves of the old hierarchy.

If caste had never been recognized in the Punjab and had never really triumphed in Magadha there would be nothing very novel in the view that salvation did not depend on it. Consequently, whether or not Buddha is accepted as an historical figure, he cannot be regarded as a popular liberator. Any idea of reforming social conditions or founding an ideal kingdom on earth was alien to early Buddhist thought. But it may well have been the anti-caste bias of the Punjabis that first gave the Buddhist order a leaning of that kind and supplied the basis of the belief that the Founder had belonged to the Kshatriya, or warrior caste. This would also explain why the Buddhist scriptures were composed, not in Sanskrit, but in the popular idiom.

There is a legend that three attempts on the life of Buddha were made by Ajatasatru, and that he succeeded in killing his own father, a Buddhist rajah. The murder was inspired by

Gotama's cousin, who has been identified with the Jainist hero, Mahavira. Later, Ajatasutra changed sides and supported the Buddhists whom he had formerly persecuted. This tradition need not be accepted literally as a fact of history, but it does suggest that from the beginning, monarchical or other political forces determined the success of the Buddhist movement. And what Ajatasutra is reputed to have begun was carried further some generations later by Chandragupta and consummated by Asoka, the grandson of Chandragupta.

Asoka found the Buddhist Order flourishing and fully established throughout his extensive kingdom. It was not, however, directly opposed to Brahmanism, though it could evidently be used to keep the latter in check. Asoka's policy was to stipulate tolerance of all religious sects and condemn their detractors. He was thus a Buddhist only in the sense that he made use of all religious organizations alike. It is doubtful whether he assimilated with more than a section of the Buddhists. Nor can we conclude that just because there is no reference to Gods and superstitious ceremonies in the edicts of Asoka, the Buddhism of his time was still comparatively pure. Edicts are not the appropriate place for such allusions. It seems certain that most of what Buddhists accept as the teaching of the Founder was penned long after the time of Asoka.

BUDDHA AS A SECONDARY GOD

We can now make a critical assessment of Buddhist origins. The Teaching Buddha, considered as the wondrous sage who established a great Order in his lifetime, shrinks to vanishing point. The suspicion that Sakyamuni is an unreal being is finally justified. The Order probably originated among ascetic Brahmins who may have been led to rationalism as a result of renouncing the Vedas. It was a monastic or mendicant sect on ordinary Brahmanist lines. To start with, it was tolerant about caste, and the tendency to diverge from Brahmanism in doctrine and practice both contributed to and encouraged its success. As an Order living under rules rather than a school of doctrine, it could include ordinary believers in the gods as well as rationalists who turned their backs on popular superstition. But the fatal obstacle to rationalism was the obtrusion of the supernatural Buddha as the source of all true wisdom, filling the role of a Secondary-god.

The very thinkers, who framed the discourses in which the Buddha employs rational argument, were nevertheless building up the belief in a supernatural being in which they themselves cannot have believed. They built worse than they knew. They relied on the popular craving for a Teaching god to spread their Order, and this frustrated the higher aims of their doctrine. The Northern Buddhists took a step from polytheism to monotheism. On the other hand, the development of the belief in a number of Buddhas, before and after Gotama, led to a return of polytheism. The places of the dethroned Gods of the Hindu pantheon were filled by five Dhyani Buddhas, mystical and divine beings living in bliss; five Bodhisatvas, or Buddhas Elect, of whom Gotama is the fourth, and Maitreya, the Buddha of Love, is still to come.

It may indeed have been the case that the Buddhists owed the success of their movement, as compared with the Jains, to their intellectual superiority. The literature of the Jains was markedly inferior and their systematic self-mortification restricted their appeal for recruits. The less ascetic Buddhists would be better able to propitiate kings and attract a popular following. This seems obvious, for example, from the maxims of the Dhammapada:

"Not nakedness, not plaited hair, not dirt, not fasting or lying on the earth, not rubbing with dust, not sitting motionless, can purify a mortal who has not overcome desires. He who, though dressed in fine apparel, exercises tranquillity, is quiet, subdued, restrained, chaste, and has ceased to find fault with all other beings, he indeed is a Brahmin, an ascetic, a fair (*bhikshu*)."

But behind such sane maxims stood forever the fabulous figure of the Buddha, the giver of all wisdom in his Order, and the imposer of its artificial rules. The mass of myths concerning him were not a late accretion to a high ethical teaching purporting to come from a normal human being. The evidence suggests, on the contrary, that the mythical figure was there first, and the ethical teaching grew up around it, even as the gospel teachings in all likelihood grew up around the name of a sacrificed Jesus who, for his early worshippers, was merely a name. No Buddha made the Buddhists — the Buddhists made the Buddha.

OBJECTIONS ANSWERED

It is reasonable to wonder why so many scholars, while admitting the tissue of fable and unplausible history surrounding the origins of Buddhism, nevertheless still believe that Sakyamuni actually existed. They usually justify their attitude by the argument that every sect must have had a founder. This assumption can be allowed if it is merely taken to mean that someone must have begun the formation of any given group. It is clearly not true in the sense that every sect originates in the new teaching of a remarkable personage.

As we have seen, there was in all probability a group of heretical Brahmanists for whom a Buddha signified "the enlightened one." Even so, there were many Buddhas before the quasi-historical Buddha had acquired a personality, like the slain Jesus of the Pauline epistles. The foundations of the Buddhist Order were Brahmanic doctrine, Brahmanic asceticism and vows, and Brahmanic mendicancy. The personal giver of the rule and teaching, the Teaching God, emerges later, just as the Jesus who institutes the Holy Supper comes after the eucharist is an established rite. Every critical scholar, without exception, admits that a vast amount of doctrine ascribed to Buddha was concocted long after his alleged period. There is not a single test whereby any of it can be shown to be genuine. There is no more psychological difficulty in supposing the whole to be doctrinal myth than in conceiving how later Brahmanists could put their discourses in the mouth of Krishna.

A sufficient nucleus for *the* Buddha lay in the general Brahmanic concept of "Buddhas." There is even a tradition that at the time when Sakyamuni came, many men ran about saying "I am the Buddha." Any fabulous Buddha as such could figure for any group as its founder to begin with. To him would be ascribed the common ethical code and rules of the group. The clothing of the phantom with the myths of Vishnu-Purusha or Krishna, the "Bhagavat" (holy teacher) of earlier creeds, followed as a matter of course on the usual lines. The quasi-biographical color given to mythical details is on the same footing with the legends of Joseph, Moses, Joshua and Jesus, all late products of secondary mythology in periods which reduced legends of the Gods to the biographical level. It is after Jesus has been deified that he is provided with a mother and a putative father and brothers; and it is in the latest gospel of all that we have some of the most circumstantial details of his life and deportment.

On these grounds it is submitted that the figure of the Buddha, in its most plausibly rationalized form, is as unhistorical as that of the gospel Jesus. Each figure shows how the religious mind manufactured a myth in a period in which the making of primary Gods had given way to the making of Secondary-gods. The mythopoeic process satisfied the craving for a Teacher-god who should originate religious and moral ideas as the earlier gods had been held to originate agriculture, art, medicine, law and civilization.

Buddhism, like Christianity, is a "failure" from the point of view of its traditional origins. In the case of Burma it admittedly did more to mold the life of the whole people towards its highest ethic than Christianity ever did; but in India, where it arose, it collapsed utterly. It was overthrown by Brahmanism which set up in its place a revived polytheism.

On our naturalistic view of the rise of the Teaching-gods, it is sheer human aspiration that has shaped all the Christs and their doctrines. One reason why the original teaching failed is that men persisted in crediting purely human aspiration to supernatural beings. Men who are taught to bow ethically to a divine Teacher are not taught ethically to think. Any aspiration so evoked is factitious, verbal, emotional, not reached by authentic thought and experience. When the wisdom or unwisdom of the nameless thinkers in all ages is recognized for what it is—as human and not divine—the nations may become capable of working out for themselves better gospels than the best of those which turned to naught in their hands while they held them as revelations from the skies.

Chapter Eight

MANES AND MANICHAEISM

Manichaeism was a quasi-Christian sect supposed to have been founded by the heresiarch, Manes. It is associated with Gnosticism, and it powerfully attracted Augustine before his conversion to orthodoxy. Its influence on Christian thought was felt long after its disappearance as an organized movement. If it could be established that Manes was indeed an historical person, this would be a striking exception to the usual process whereby a mythical founder evolves from a cult, like Buddha, Jesus and other Teaching-gods.

What do we know of the life of Manes? The alleged biographical material is derived from both Christian and Persian sources. The Christian tradition runs that one Scythianus, a Saracen, husband of an Egyptian woman, "introduced the doctrine of Empedocles and Pythagoras into Christianity;" that he had a disciple, "Buddas, formerly named Terebinthus"; who travelled in Persia, where he alleged that he had been born of a virgin, and afterwards wrote four books, one of Mysteries, a second The Gospel, a third The Treasure, and a fourth Heads. While performing some mystic rites, he was hurled down a precipice by a daimon, and killed. A woman at whose house he lodged buried him, took over his property and bought a boy of seven, named Cubricus. This boy she freed and educated, leaving him the property and books of Buddas-Terebinthus. Cubricus then travelled into Persia, where he took the name of Manes and gave forth the doctrines of Buddas-Terebinthus as his own. The King of Persia (not named), hearing that he worked miracles, sent for him to heal his sick son, and on the child's dying put Manes in prison. He escaped into Mesopotamia, but was traced, captured, and flayed alive by the Persian King's orders, the skin being then stuffed with chaff and hung up before the gate of the city.

For this narrative the historian Socrates, writing in the fifth century, gives as his authority "The Disputation (with Manes) of Archelaus bishop of Caschar," a work either unknown to or disregarded by Eusebius, who in his History briefly vilifies Manes without giving any of the above details. In the Chronicon of Eusebius, the origin of the sect is placed in the second year of Probus, A.D. 277, but this passage is probably from the hand of Jerome. According to Jerome, Archelaus wrote his account of his "Disputation with Manichaeus" in Syriac, whence it was translated into Greek. The Greek is lost, and the work, apart from extracts, subsists only in a Latin translation from the Greek, of doubtful age and fidelity, probably made after the fifth century. By Photius it is stated that Heraclean, bishop of Chalcedon, in his book against the Manichaeans, said the (Greek) Disputation of Archelaus was written by one Hegemonius—an author not otherwise traceable, and of unknown date.

In the Latin narrative, "Manes" is said to have come, after his flight from court, from Arabion, a frontier fortress, to Caschar or Carchar, a town said to be in Roman Mesopotamia, in the hope of converting an eminent Christian there, named Marcellus, to whom he had sent a letter beginning: "Manichaeus, apostle of Jesus Christ, and all the saints and virgins with me, send peace to Marcellus." In his train he brought twenty-two (or twelve) youths and virgins. At the request of Marcellus, he debated on religion with bishop Arcelaus, by whom he was vanquished; whereupon he set out to return to Persia. On his way he proposed to debate with a priest at the town of Diodorides, but Archelaus came to take the priest's place, and again defeated him; whereupon, fearing to be given up to the Persians by the Christians, he returned to Arabion.

At this stage Archelaus introduces, in a discourse to the people, his history of "this Manes," very much to the effect of the recapitulation in Socrates. Among the further details are these: (1) Scythianos lived "in the time of the Apostles." (2) Terebinthus said the name of Buddas had been imposed on him. (3) In the mountains he had been brought up by an angel. (4) He had been convicted of imposture by a Persian prophet named Parcus, and by Labadcus, son of Mithra. (5) In the disputation he taught concerning the sphere, the two luminaries, the transmigration of souls, and the war of the "Principia" against God. (6) Cubricus, about the age of sixty, translated the books of Terebinthus. (7) He made three chief disciples, Thomas, Addas, and Hermas, of whom he sent the first to Egypt, and the second to Scythia, keeping the third with him. (8) The two former returned when he was in prison, and he sent them to procure for him the books of the Christians, which he then studied. According to the Latin narrative, finally, Manes on his return to Arabion was seized and taken to the Persian king, by whose orders he was flayed, his body being left to the birds, and his skin, filled with air, hung at the city gate.

That this narrative is historically worthless is admitted by all critical students; and recent historians turn from the Christian to the oriental accounts of the heresiarch for a credible view. There "Mani" is described as a painter, who set up a sectarian movement in opposition to Zoroastrianism, which was then in renewed favor in Persia, in the reign of Shapur I. Being proceeded against, he fled to Turkestan, where he made disciples and embellished with paintings a Tchighil (Chinese name for a temple) and another temple called Ghalbita. Provisioning in advance a cave which had a spring, he told his disciples he was going to heaven, and would not return for a year, after which time they were to seek him in the cave in question. There they found him, whereupon he showed them an illustrated book, called Ergenk, or Estenk, which he said he had brought from heaven. He then had many followers, with whom he returned to Persia at the death of Shapur.

The new king, Hormisdas, joined and protected the sect, and built Mani a castle. The next king, Bahram or Varanes, at first favored Mani, but, after getting him to debate with certain Zoroastrian teachers, caused him to be flayed alive, and the skin to be stuffed and hung up as alleged by the Christians. Thereupon most of his followers fled to India, and some even to China, those remaining being reduced to slavery.

In yet another Mohammedan account, we have the details that Mani's mother was named Meis or Utachin, or Mar Marjam (Sancta Maria) and that he was supernaturally born. At the behest of an angel he began his public career, at the age of twenty-four with two companions, on a Sunday, the first day of Nisan, when the sun was in Aries. He travelled for about forty years; wrote *six* books. and was raised to Paradise after being slain under Bahram, "son of Shapur." Some say he was crucified "in two halves" and so hung up at two gates, afterwards called High-Mani and Low-Mani; others say that he was imprisoned by Shapur and freed by Bahram; others hold that he died in prison. "But he was certainly crucified."

Thus the sole detail which the Mohammedan and Christian writers have in common is that of the execution with its exemplary sequel.

Both accounts, it will be observed, make Mani an innovating heretic, but the Persian treats him as inventing his doctrine, while the Christian makes it traditive. The Persian story, however, makes him compose and illustrate his book in Turkestan, with the possible implication that such a book was a novelty in Persia, despite Mani's profession. Baur and Neander, accordingly, combining the Christian clue of the name Buddas with the Persian clue to Turkestan, infer that in that territory Mani acquired a knowledge of Buddhism.

To this solution, however, there are several objections. In the first place, there are in Manichaeism only shadowy analogies to Buddhism; in the second, the name Buddas is plausibly interpreted as being merely a Greek corruption of Butm or Budm, the Chaldaic name of the terebinth tree—a simple translation of Terebinthus. On the other hand, Ritter has conjectured that "Terebinthus" may be a corruption of Buddha's title, "Tere Hintu," Lord of the Hindus. Finally, it has to be noted that Herodotus repeatedly mentions a people called the Budini, among whom were settled the Neuri, who "seem to be magicians," so that "Buddas" might be a reminiscence of their repute. We have thus a pleasing variety of choices!

THE MANICHAEAN SOLUTION

Seeking for a solution, we may assume that whatever tradition the Christians had concerning Manes they got from the east, and it is conceivable that from the datum of Turkestan they evolved the ideas of "Scythianus" and "Buddas," with or without the help of the knowledge that "Budh" might stand for "Terebinthus" in Chaldea. But the Persian tradition in itself has little weight, being merely a way of saying that Mani's doctrine had associations with other lands. On the face of the story, he was heretical before he left Persia, and the medley of theosophical doctrines associated with Manichaeism can be traced on the one hand to the general storehouse of Babylonian lore, whence came the lore of Christian Gnosticism, and on the other hand to Mazdaism.

Such an amalgamation could very well take place on the frontiers of the Persian and Roman empires, early in the Christian era. But it has to be asked how and why Manichaeism, which at so many points resembles the Gnostic systems so-called, should have held its ground as a cult while they were suppressed. Its Jesus and Christ were as far as theirs from conforming to the doctrines of the Church, and it was furiously persecuted for centuries. The explanation apparently lies in the element of cultus, in the exaltation of the Founder. Was this then a case in which an abnormal Teacher really founded a religion by his doctrine and the force of his personality?

In order to form an opinion we have first to note two outstanding features of Manichaeism—the doctrine that Manichaeus was "the Paraclete;" and the fact that his quasi-crucifixion was devoutly commemorated by his devotees in the Bema festival at the season of the Christian Easter. Concerning the datum, the most significant consideration is that the equivalence of the names Mani or Manes and Manichaeus is to be explained only on the theory that they are both variants of an Eastern name equivalent to the Hebrew name *Menahem*, which has in part the same meaning as Paraclete. Seeing that Manes is declared to have called himself the Paraclete promised in the Christian gospel, the question arises whether he was in Syria called Menahem (—*Manichaios*) on this account, or whether Mani was for Persians, as was Manes or Mane for Greeks and Romans, a passable equivalent for Menahem, in which the third consonant was a guttural. And seeing that the same name is Graecized as Manaen in the Book of Acts, this appears to be the fact.

Now, the name Menahem, being formed from the root *nahem*, is often translated in the Septuagint as "the Comforter." It has not in Hebrew the various senses of advocate, mediator, messenger and intercessor, conveyed by *parakletos*, but there are some reasons for holding that in post-Biblical use it may have had a similar significance with the Greek term. In particular, we find it in late Judaic lore practically identified with the title of Messiah, the Messiah Ben-David being called the Menakhem Ben-Ammiel; while the Messiah Ben-Joseph is named Nehemia Ben-Uziel. The Talmud brings the identification in close touch with Jesuism: "R. Joshua ben Levi saith, His name is tsemach, 'A Branch' " (Zech. III, 8. *Tsemach* it will be remembered—Netzer). "R. Juda Bar Aibu saith, His name is Menahem." Jesus, it will be remembered, becomes the *parakletos* in the sense of an intercessor, being yet at the same time an atonement. And if there is reason to refer the doctrine of the two Messiahs to an extra-Judaic source, a similar surmise is permissible as to the two Menahems.

In this connection we have next to note that the story of Mani's concealment in the cave is a strikingly close parallel to the old story in Herodotus concerning the reputed Thracian God Zalmoxis or Zamolxis, of whom "some think that he is the same with Gebelezeis."

"Every fifth year they despatch one of themselves, taken by lot, to Zálmoxis, with orders to let him know on each occasion what they want. Their mode of sending him is this. Some of them are appointed to hold three javelins; while others, having taken up the man . . . by the hands and feet, swing him round, and throw him into the air upon the points. If he should die, being transfixed, they think the God is propitious to them; if he should not die, they blame the *messenger* himself, saying that he is a bad man, and having blamed him they despatch another."

Gebelezeis may be the Babylonian Fire-God Gibil, identified with Nusku. In that case, the sacrifice to him of a messenger is one more instance of sacrificing the God to himself, as Gibil-Nusku was the messenger of all the Gods. According to the Greeks of the Hellespont and Pontus, Zalmoxis was a man who had been a slave, at Samos, to Pythagoras, son of Mmesarchus; then was freed, became rich, and retired to his own country, Thrace, where he taught the doctrine of immortality. While teaching this in a dwelling he caused to be built, "he in the meantime had an underground dwelling made, and when the building was finished he vanished from among the Thracians, and having gone down to the underground dwelling he abode there three years." In the fourth year he reappeared to the Thracians, who had deemed him dead, and thus his teaching became credible to them. Herodotus, "neither disbelieving nor entirely believing" the legend, was "of opinion that this Zalmoxis lived many years before Pythagoras;" and we, in turn, seeing in the story of the three years' stay underground a remote form of the myth of the God-man's three days in the grave, pronounce that the legends of the freed slave Mani and his concealment in the cave are of similar antiquity.

He is the *Menahem* or messenger of the cult of the Thracian Getae; and in another "Scythian" record we have a clue to the legend of his death, as well as to the myth of "Scythianos." The flaying of slain enemies was a Scythian usage; and "many, having flayed men whole, and stretched the skin on wood, carry it about on horseback." As with the enemy, so with the "messenger" whose function is a recognized one in barbaric sacrifice. At the death of a king, they strangled and buried one of his concubines, a cupbearer, a cook, a groom, a page, a courier, and horses, and "firstlings of everything else." A year later they strangled fifty of his young men-servants and fifty of the finest horses and, having disembowelled them, *stuffed them with chaff* and sewed them up. The bodies of the horses were then transfixed and mounted on horses, and the whole ghastly cavalcade moved round the "high-place" made over the king's grave. An evolution of such funerary honorific sacrifices into sacrifices to the Gods is in the normal way of religious history. In Dahomey again, it was *de rigueur* in modern times that every occurrence at court should be reported to the spirit of the king's father by a male or female messenger, who was commonly though not always sacrificed.

The Thracian Getae, who carried on the cult of Zalmoxis and the ritually slain messenger, were subdued by Darius, and embodied in his empire, with other Scythian tribes, and in that vast aggregate their sacrificial rites had the usual chance of being adopted by their conquerors—if indeed they were not already associated with the worship of Gibil-Nusku the Babylonian Fire-god, and so known to the Persian fire-worshippers. And, whether or not by way of such an adoption, we find that after the death of the captive Emperor Valerain, his skin was *dyed red and stuffed with straw*, and was so preserved for centuries in the chief temple of Persia—a course strongly suggestive of religious symbolism.

By certain Arab tribes, who worshipped the planet Mars, a warrior in bloodstained garments was annually sacrificed by being thrown into a pit, and the God was worshipped in a temple of red color—a kindred conception. Such a proceeding as the Persian, in fact, would have been impossible in a temple without religious precedent; and in the sacrificial practices of the pre-Christian Mexicans, which can be traced back to an ancient Asiatic center, we find clear duplicates of both details of the quasi-sacrifice of Valerian, together with the messenger-sacrifices of the Khonds and Getae. On the one hand, it is recorded that the Mexican "knights of the sun" on a certain day sacrificed to the Sun a human victim whom they smeared all over with some red substance. "They sent him to the Sun with the message . . . that his Knights remained at his service, and gave him infinite thanks for the great . . . favors bestowed on them in the wars."

So, again, in the sacrifice to Xiuhteuctli the Fire-god in the tenth month the victims were painted red. On the other hand, in a great annual festival held on the last day of the first month, in which a hundred slaves were sacrificed, some were flayed, and their skins were worn in a religious dance by leading devotees, among them being the king. Finally the bodies were sacramentally eaten, and the skins, "filled with cotton-wool, or straw" were "hung in the temple and king's palace for a memorial." The stuffed skin of the victim, then, was sacrosanct, and that which had been worn by the king was doubtless specially so, representing as it did at once the deified victim and the monarch. When the king took a captive in war with his own hands, the latter was specially regarded as the representative of the sun, and was clothed with the Sun-god's royal insignia. As for the red-painting of the messenger sent to the sun, that in turn was presumably a special symbolical identification of the victim with the God, as in the peculiar Peruvian sacrifice of a shorn sheep "in a red waistcoat" to the Sun-god at Cuzco. The final inference is that the dead or slain body of the captive Emperor Valerian was made to figure as a sacrificial special messenger sent by the Persian king to the (messenger) Sun-god, and dedicated to that deity.

THE MYTH OF MANES

That the legendary "crucifixion" of "Manichaeus" was a myth derived from such a sacrifice is the more probable, in view of the evolution of the Christian mystery drama from an analogous rite. Clemens Alexandrinus, following another authority than Herodotus, tells how "a barbarous nation, not cumbered with philosophy, select, it is said, *annually* an ambassador to the hero Zamolxis," choosing one held to be *of special virtue*. The usage would thus seem to have made headway after the time of Herodotus. Clemens, too, identifies with Zoroaster that Er, son of Armenius, who in Plato figures as "the messenger from the other world," having gone thither in a death swoon. This suggests that the Persians now connected the doctrine of immortality with some conception or usage resembling that of the Getae, and that Zoroaster, in turn, was mythically associated with a cave containing flowers and fountains, the whole symbolical of the world, and further associated with resurrection in the mysteries. Finally, the Manichaeans' annual celebration of the Bema—their name for the rite commemorative of the death of Manichaeus—carries with it no explanation, and must be taken as the title of some Graeco-Oriental mystery-ritual. The word signifies "platform," referring not to the ordinary Bema of the Christian churches, wherein stood the altar, but to the covered platform of five steps prepared by the Manichaean devotees on the anniversary of the Founder's death, though it is not accounted for by any item in the legendary biography, where no such platform is mentioned.

Upon the platform described by Augustine, something must have been represented or enacted, and as he appears never to have been one of the *electi*, but only an auditor or catechumen, he would be, as the Manichaeans declared, unacquainted with the special mysteries of the system. The "five steps" point to a symbol of the proto-Chaldean high-place or temple-pyramid and altar of sacrifice, often of five stages, and the mystery was in all likelihood akin to the early mystery-drama of the Christian crucifixion. The apparent identification of the birthday of Manichaeus, in the late Mohammedan account, with the death-day in the known cultus, and further the symbolism of his public appearances "with two others," suggest a mystic scene analogous to the triple crucifixion. In any case, the graded or terraced pyramid, which was at once the norm of a sacrificial altar and the norm of the temples of Babylonia, Mexico and the South Sea Islands, was also the norm of regal tombs, as instanced by that of Cyrus, still extant.

The critical presumption, then, is that the flayed and stuffed Manichaeus is one more figure created out of a rite of annual sacrifice, and that the Manichaean cult is no more the invention of a man named Manes than is the Buddhist the work of one founder. The works ascribed to Mani, so far as known, have every mark of being late concoctions, on Gnostic lines, framed for purposes of proselytism in the Christian sphere, each purporting to be written by "Manichaeus, an apostle of Jesus Christ," in the manner of the Christian epistles. The "Epistle to the Virgin Menoch," of which fragments are preserved by Augustine in the *Opus Imperfectum*, suggests anew the special significance of the title Manichaeus. As for the *Erteng* or *Erzeng*, specially associated in Persia with the name of Mani, the title, it appears, simply means an illustrated book; and such a book is no more to be supposed primordial in the cult than the epistles.

The success of the cult, in fine, was attained very much as was that of Christism. Its promoters, early recognizing the vital importance of organization, created a system of twelve chief apostles or *magistri*, with a leader, representing the Founder, and seventy-two bishops, here copying actual Judaism rather than Christian tradition. Despite its discouragement of marriage and procreation, the cult survived centuries of murderous persecution in the Eastern empire; finally passing on to the West through the later sects affected by its tradition—the germs of a new heresy in the Middle Ages. Like the crucified Christ, as we have seen reason to think, its Founder was an imaginary being, and so it outlasted the tough sects of Marcion and Montanus, of which the latter was all but victorious against orthodoxy. Montanus, says one record, claimed to be inspired by the Paraclete, and his movement, being organized on ecclesiastical lines, went far, beginning in Phrygia, where, as in Persia, the doctrine of a Paraclete was probably pre-Christian.

That Montanus in turn was an imaginary personage is plausibly argued by Schwegler, but though some of the adherents of the sect seem to have tended to make of him the Paraclete, it appears to have been a fanatical movement founded on no particular personality, being more commonly named Phrygian than Montanist, from its place of origin, and offering no analogies to Manichaeism save in respect of a general asceticism. Being rather a special development of tendencies already present in the Christian movement than a new creed, it had less lasting power than the other, though its vogue and duration were sufficient to prove how much of what passes for a new religious development to Christianity was but the exploitation of elements of ecstatic and ascetic fanaticism abundantly present in the old pagan environment, of which Phrygia was a typical part.

Chapter Nine

APOLLONIUS AND JESUS

Before investigating the historicity of other Saviors and Teachers to whom divine honors have been paid, it is necessary to clear up a possible misconception. The view I have advanced does not imply that wherever legends have grown up around some notable personage there is nothing except legend. There are many historical characters whose real existence we have no reason to doubt in spite of the fact that their life story is encrusted with fable. In the Middle Ages, myths were connected with Charlemagne, Theodoric and Virgil, but they were undoubtedly historical characters. Perhaps the same could be said of Solomon.

It is not the ascription of prodigies to some remarkable man that leads us to doubt his reality. Each case must be considered on its merits when we apply the tests of historical evidence. We must distinguish between what the imagination has added to a meager biography, and those cases in which the biography itself has been added to what has grown out of a ritual or doctrine. We have seen how Jesus grew out of a mystery-play, and how Buddha became attached to an already existing body of teaching. This is a very different process from the accumulation of miracles and tales about a real person. The difference is illustrated by the case of Apollonius of Tyana.

Apollonius lived in the first century of our era. By the third century a wealth of legend surrounded his name. He was believed to have had a supernatural birth, to have worked many miracles, to have made disciples and converts in Europe and Asia, and finally to have ascended to heaven. He has been plausibly described as a "Pagan Christ." Superficially the resemblance may seem striking. If these prodigies may be told of an actual man, it may be asked, why may not Jesus be actual, of whom similar prodigies are told?

The answer is that prodigies in themselves are not enough to make us doubt his existence. The abundant attribution of miracles to Apollonius soon after his own day shows what little value can be placed on miracle stories as certificates of divinity. The credulity of the Fathers of the Church is proved by the fact that they did not deny the truth of the wonders Apollonius was said to perform. To the early Christians these marvels were accepted, but explained as the work of demons.

They never thought of testing whether Apollonius was a real person. There is, however, no reason for us to suspect an invention, save as regards the details of the biography recast by Philostratus in the third century. It is likely enough that he was a devout Pythagorean, a student of medicine and astrology, a universalist in his creed, and a believer in immortality. He may conceivably have travelled in India, though there are no details available.

Such contemporary testimony as has survived is preserved in the "Life" written by Philostratus. According to this account, Apollonius died in the reign of Nerva (96–98 A.D.). The first incidental traces of his fame are in Dio Cassius' History of Rome, where he is mentioned as a miraculous seer, and in Origen's reply to Celsus. Origen cites one, Moiragenes, who is also mentioned by Philostratus, as having referred to the accounts of magical feats in the memoirs of Apollonius. It is stated that some philosophers were convinced by them. These references belong to the very period of the production of the "Life" by Philostratus, so that there is no trace of any impression previously made by the memoirs of Damis and Maximus of Aegae, declared to be used by him. Still, we have no reason for doubting that there was an Apollonius of Tyana, who made an impression in his day as a wandering teacher, and perhaps as a sorcerer, and whose memory was preserved by statues in several towns, as well as by one or two memoirs, one of them written by his credulous or mendacious disciple, Damis. Of the large number of letters preserved as his—some of them remarkable for their terse force—it is impossible to be sure that they are genuine, though they may very well be so.

The reason for not doubting on the main point is that it was a much easier matter to take a known name as a nucleus for a mass of marvels and teachings than to build it up, as the phrase goes about the cannon, "round a hole." The difference between such a case and those of Jesuism and Buddhism is obvious. In those cases, there was a cultus and an organization to be accounted for, and a biography of the Founder had to be forthcoming. In the case of Apollonius, despite the string of marvels attached to his name, there was no cultus. Posterity was interested in him as it was in Pythagoras or Plato. Philostratus undertook the recasting of the "Life" in literary form at the command of the empress Julia Domna, a great eclectic. Even if, as has been so often argued, there was an original intention to set off Apollonius against Jesus, we should not have ground to doubt that a teaching Apollonius had flourished in the first century; rather the assumption would be that the pagans would seek for some famous wonder-worker whose life they could manipulate.

ALLEGED ECHO OF THE GOSPELS

But there is really no reason to suppose that Philostratus, much less Damis, had the gospels before him, though he may well have heard of their story. A close comparison of the story of the raising of Jairus' daughter with the story in Philostratus, to which it is so closely parallel, gives rather reason to believe that the gospels copied the pagan narrative. The gospel story was unmentioned by Arnobius and Lactantius in lists in which they ought to have given it had they known and accepted it. The story, however, was probably told of other thaumaturgs before Apollonius, and in regard to the series of often strained parallels drawn by Baur, as by Huet, it may confidently be said that, instead of their exhibiting any calculated attempt to outdo or cap the gospel narratives, they stand for the general taste of the time in thaumaturgy. Apollonius, like Jesus, casts out devils and heals the sick, and if the "Life" were a parody of the gospel, we should expect him to give sight to the blind. This, however, is not the case, and on the other hand the gospel story of the healing of two blind men is certainly a duplicate of a pagan record.

To say, as does Baur,[1] that the casting-out of devils in the Apollonian legend is necessarily an echo of the gospels, on the score that the Greek and Roman literatures at that time show no traces of the idea, is to make the arbitrary assumption that the superstitions of Syria could enter the West only by Judaic or Christian channels. The "Metamorphoses" of Apuleius, to say nothing of those of Ovid, might serve to remind us that the empire imbibed the *diablerie* of the East at every pore, and the wizardry of Apollonius includes many Eastern items of which the gospels show no trace. As for the annunciation of the birth of Apollonius by Proteus, and the manner of its happening, they conform alike to Egyptian myths and to that told concerning the birth of Plato. It is, in fact, the Christian myth that draws upon the common store of Greek and Syrian myth, not the Apollonian legend that borrows from the Christian.

The descent of Apollonius to Hades, again, seems to have been alleged, after common Graeco-Asiatic precedent, before the same myth became part of the Christian dogmatic code, and to say that his final disappearance without dying and his apparition afterwards must have been motived by the story of Christ's appearance to Saul is once more to ignore the whole lesson of comparative hierology. Baur goes so far as to argue that when Philostratus says the disciples of Apollonius in Greece were called Apollonians, he must be merely framing a parallel to the title of the Christians, because there is *now* no knowledge of a sect of Apollonians. It was very hard, several generations ago, for even a great scholar to realize the broadest laws of religious evolution. Yet Lardner[2] had shown with reasonable force, in his primitive fashion, nearly a century before, that the model before Philostratus, if there be any, is not Jesus but Pythagoras, and his friend De la Roche had rightly and tersely summed up the whole case in the words: "Philostratus said nothing more in the Life of Apollonius than he would have said if there had been no Christians in the world." For once, Baur had not fully grappled with the literature of his subject. His superiority to

[1]*Apollonius von Tyana und Christus* (1832).
[2]Works ed 1835. vi 489 seq.

his Christian predecessors as a critic of Apollonius comes out chiefly in his gravely candid recognition of the high moral purpose set forth in all the discourses ascribed to the hero in the "Life."

The habit of pitting Apollonius against Jesus really arose about a century after Philostratus, when the pagan intelligence first began to feel itself menaced by the new creed. Hierocles set the fashion in his *Philalethes Logos*, to which Eusebius and Lactantius replied in the normal patristic manner. A hundred years later still, in the time of Augustine, the setting of the miracles of Apollonius and Apuleius against those of Jesus was a common line of pagan argument, met in the usual way, neither side convincing the other. If there was any gain it was on the pagan side, for while Chrysostom triumphs over the failure of the Apollonian movement, such a classically cultured Christian bishop as Sidonius Apollinaris acclaims the personal virtues and philosophic teaching of the pagan sage. The pagans on their part had taken him up all round.

In the time of Philostratus, Alexander Severus had eclectically placed a bust of Apollonius, with others of Abraham, Jesus, and Orpheus, in his private chapel or oratory, and later we find Eunapius, Ammianus Marcellinus, Vopiscus, and Apuleius, from their different standpoints treating the Tyanean as a demi-god, or divinely inspired, or a supreme Mage.

MIRACLES NOT ENOUGH

It was not, of course, the high ethic and philosophy of the Apollonian discourses that they stressed against the Christians. Such a saying as "I have found my reward in the amendment of men" was not a word to conjure with in popular debate. It was the miracles, the prodigies, the fables, that were for ancient readers the warrant of the sage's greatness. Today we cannot tell any more than they to what extent the remarkable discourses which Philostratus professes to copy from Damis stand for any genuine utterances or writings of Apollonius; we can be satisfied of the historicity of the man without knowing how far to trust the accounts of his travels and teaching. But we know that if Apollonius had uttered every wise or eloquent teaching put in his mouth by his biographers, he could not thereby have founded such a cult as the Christians conducted on the basis of an entirely fictitious biography.

Lactantius, in the patristic style, asks Hierocles: "Why therefore, O mad head, doth none worship Apollonius for a God, unless perchance thou alone, worthy indeed of that God, with whom the true God will punish thee to all eternity?" We today can give the answer of hierology. No man was ever deified for his wisdom, or even for his supposed miracles; religions grow up around rites offered immemorially to unknown powers, or round ways of life set up by generations of nameless teachers, all of which abstractions alike take form as named Gods or Sons of Gods. In one age they are the givers of civilization, agriculture, knowledge, crafts, arts, rites, and laws, and in another of oracles, of revelations, of doctrines and discourses, of their own lives as redeemers. But the really slain man, the true human sacrifice, though he be counted by millions, is not deified; not he, but an abstraction shaped out of the mystic drama and sacrament which have followed on ages of sacrifices and sacraments of human flesh, and neither is the true teacher or thinker deified; not he, but a superposed abstraction distilled from many teachings, wise and unwise, put by many generations in the mouth of the mythical one. For it is by such modes alone that men have been able to create the economic bases without which no religion can live. Apollonius, credited with many miracles and wondrous wisdom, like Pythagoras long before him, could become a God only by way of a passing figure of speech, precisely because he had really lived and taught.

Given the culture-stage in which many crave the Teaching-god, while the multitude still crave the Sacrificed-god, a cult which combines these in one Deity, still retaining the cosmic Creator-god and adding the attractive appeal of the Mother-goddess, has obviously a maximum chance of survival. And such a religion, we have seen reason to conclude, cannot be founded on concrete personages; it must be developed from personalized abstractions. Such a combination is presented in the Christian cultus. But all such success is finally in terms of political and economic adaptations. The final explanation of non-survivals, accordingly, is to be found in the lack or frustration of such adaptations. It remains to note, then, how some systems historically developed from abstractions, like the Christian, have disappeared in the struggle for existence.

Chapter Ten

THE EVOLUTION OF MITHRA

In the early centuries of the Christian era Mithraism was the most nearly universal religion of the Western world. The monumental remains of the Roman period show its extraordinary extension in almost all parts of the empire. In Britain among the monuments found in a Mithraic cave at Housesteads, in Northumberland, containing sculptures is an inscription: "To the God, best and greatest, invincible Mithra, Lord of Ages." Another, at Chichester, bears the inscription: "To the God, the Sun, the invincible Mithra, the Lord of the Ages." There are other monuments at Chester, Oxford, York, Manchester, and London. In Germany and France a number of Mithraic bas-reliefs have been found, and monuments of various kinds abound in the Alps, Eastern Italy, Dalmatia and many Mediterranean ports. The distribution is unequal, but it is clear that the cult went with the legions and the Syrian traders who followed them.

Yet in spite of the evidence that Mithraism was the most widespread of the religious systems of the Roman Empire, the cult seems to have been forgotten in Europe for a thousand years. After the time of the Church Fathers, for whom Mithraism was a most serious thorn in the flesh, there is no mention of it in European literature until the late fifteenth century. Ignorance of the subject was so complete, even among scholars, that of three now well-known Mithraic monuments discovered in the sixteenth century, not one was attributed to Mithra. The famous group so often engraved of Mithra slaying the bull was thought to represent Jupiter carrying off Europa.

In searching for the origin of Mithraism, it is necessary to examine some of the older systems, since all religions are phases of a continuous evolution. In the earliest Aryan documents, the Vedas, Mitra, or Mithra may have been to begin with a special epithet of the sun. "Mithra is greater than the earth and the sky; he supports even all the gods," we read in the Rig Veda (iii, 59, 7–8). He is frequently associated with Varuna and Agni. According to the Atharva Veda, "In the evening he becomes Varuna Agni; in the morning he becomes Mitra going forth"—an expression that plainly points to the Sun-god. However, in India the pre-Aryan Agni instead of Mithra gained preeminence, whereas the Mithra cult developed in Aryan Persia. What remains of the ancient lore of Mithraism is contained in the Iranian *Zend Avesta*. The title of this compilation is somewhat misleading, since *Zend* does not signify a language, as was formerly supposed, but a commentary or explanation; and *Avesta* is the proper name of the original texts.

The religion of the *Avesta* is commonly called Mazdean from the divine name Ahura Mazda. In the later portions of the Avesta, the Mithra cult is closely associated with Zoroaster (or Zarathustra). There are no good grounds for supposing Zoroaster to have been a real person. Even those who believe that he was an historical figure admit that not a single biographical detail has been found. The religious dualism attributed to him is in all likelihood a natural adaptation by priests of a polytheistic process of thought. It seems far more probable that "Zarathustra" was an ancient title for a kind of priest-king than that there was a man so named who invented monotheistic dualism, even as Abraham is fabled to have discovered monotheism, and somehow succeeded in imposing his doctrine as a system of ritual and worship on his contemporaries.

Zoroastrianism and Mithraism were certainly not originally one; neither did one grow out of the other, though they may have been fused by some conquest. For a time—and this suggests Zoroastrian influence—Mithra was graded as the subordinate of Ahura-Mazda. Although in the Vedas, Mitra and Varuna enjoy equal powers and are paired, in the *Avesta*, Ahura-Mazda cannot bear an equal. The ritual makes this clear: "We sacrifice unto Mithra, the lord of all countries, whom Ahura-Mazda made the most glorious of all the Gods in the world unseen." Mithra is one of the supreme God's creations, but he occupied nonetheless the highest position. He was God of the heavenly light, of the vast luminous spaces, of the wide pastures above. He was invoked as the God of battles, swift to slay the enemies of truth and justice—i.e. the enemies of his worshippers. Thus we have the cultus of Mithra, as the Sun-god, the deity of light and truth, fighting on the side of good against the evil power, Angra-Mainyu (Ahriman), long before Christianity.

Apart from the Avesta the bulk of the literature of Mazdaism perished in the Arab conquest. We can only infer the nature of the rest of the system. But we do know that Mithra came to occupy a place only a little inferior to that of Ahura-Mazda. Artaxerxes Mnemon (d. B.C. 358) placed an image of Mithra in the temple attached to the royal palace of Suza. In his inscriptions he unites Mithra with Ahura Mazda and prays for their conjoint protection. He swore by "the light of Mithra" as our William the Conquerer swore by "the splendor of God." The importance and range of Mithraic worship can be judged from the mere vogue of the name Mithridates, "the justice of Mithra," at least six hundred years before the Christian era.

It is after the Persian conquest of Babylon (538 B.C.) that Mithraism begins to take the shape it wears in the period of the Roman Empire. We may say that the Mazdeism of the Persians united with the astrolatry of the Chaldeans and produced Mithraism. Before this development Mazdeism had entered Armenia about 625 B.C., but the older Mazdean deity was in some measure superseded by Mithra. Mithraism was prepared in Armenia for its cosmopolitan career in the Western world. It borrowed from Armenian Mazdeism the enigmatic supreme God, "Kronos Zervan," the Time Spirit. This is a Babylonian conception, represented in the mysteries by the lion-headed or demon-headed and serpent-encircled figure which bears the two keys for the two locked doors of exit and entrance in the firmament.

THE SAVIOR-GOD

We must not exclude the possibility that certain features of Mithraism derive equally with those of Babylonian cults from a common source of great antiquity. Mithra partly equates with Bel or Enlil, originally a War-god, known as "lord of lands," even as Mithra is "lord of wide pastures" and "all countries" and a bearer of "glorious weapons." These seem to be early and not late attributes of Mithra. Bel gives place to Merodach (Marduk) who becomes the Mediator-god, but this evolution in Mithra's case may follow older lines.

New Year's day is the festival of Bel, Merodach and Mithra. The Babylonian War-god and Sun-god Shamas, a prototype of the Hebrew Samson, was Judge and Savior of all men and the destroyer of the wicked. Mithra had all these attributes and was identified with Shamas, but not necessarily modelled on him as the underlying concept is earlier than both cults. On the other hand, when Mithra absorbs in himself the idea of the Logos, we may suppose that the adaptation is late.

Of the deity thus shaped through many centuries by many forces it may be said that his cult was ethically advanced in comparison with contemporary worships. In remote times no doubt he received human sacrifices, like most other Gods. The Persian practice of sacrificing on a high-place tells of early connection with the Asiatic cult of pyramid-altar-temples which spread to Polynesia, North America, Syria and Greece, always in connection with sacrifices of men and children. But there is no trace of this practice in the historical period, and at no time do we find any trace in the legend of sexual complications. Unlike Agni, unlike Krishna, Apollo, Adonis, Heracles, Dionysus and Attis, Mithra has no amours. His conjunction with Anaitis (or Anahid) seems to have been a mystical blending of sexes rather than a conjugal union. His mate seems to have been primarily Ardivisura, a Goddess of a sacred well and earth-waters, later blended with the Semitic Anahid, Goddess of fruitfulness. At times he may have been licentiously worshipped as Anaitis was, but in the *Avesta*, and later, he is always shown as making for righteousness.

Originally Mithra was simply the animized Sun; later, according to the universal law of religious evolution, he became a spirit apart from the sun, but symbolized by it. In Persian his name (Mihr) actually means the sun; the same word also means "the friend." The light being the friend of man seems to connote love or amity, and a moral distinction attaches to Mithra at a period when words have incalculable significance. He is not a mere benefactor to be flattered. The Sun can both succor and slay. Just as Pindar called Apollo the most friendly to men of all the gods although he is also the Destroyer, so the Persians sang: "Thou, O Mithra, art both bad and good to nations."

At length Mithra came to occupy the position of Mediator between the two great powers of good and evil, Ormazd and Ahriman. To the devout eye he appeared as a humane and beneficent God, a savior and redeemer, eternally young, son of the Most High, preserver of mankind from the Evil One. In brief, he is a pagan Christ.

Much has been written as to whether Mithra was worshipped as the sun or as the creator and sustainer of the sun. There can be no doubt that the two ideas existed and were often blended. We may be sure that for weak and ignorant minds, which could conceive a personal God only under the form of a man or animal, or both combined, the perpetual pageant of the sun was a help and not a hindrance to elevation of thought. We can understand, too, how even to thinkers who regarded the sun only as a material universe it should nevertheless be the very symbol of life and splendor and immortality; and that it should be the chosen seat of the deity who ruled mankind. The viewless spirit of the sun was believed to proclaim to man the oracle of the Soul of the Universe: "I am the Alpha and the Omega, the first and the last, which is, and which was, and which is to come, the Almighty."

THE SLAYER OF THE BULL

In the great polytheistic era, the habit of personifying the forces of nature led at first to a universal recognition of the existence of the Gods of foreign peoples, and later to the idea that all these Gods are but names of phases of one central and omnipotent Power. Even among philosophers and theologians this conception never really destroyed the habit of thinking of the manifestations of *the* God as being minor deities. The synthesizing tendency, however, led to different cults being combined and different god-names being identified as referring to the same God. Also various Gods were combined in unities of two, three, four or more members. Egypt is the great theological factory for such combinations, but the law operated elsewhere.

The conception of a Divine Trinity is of unknown antiquity. It flourished in Mesopotamia, India, Egypt, and in Platonic philosophy long before Christianity. The combining process had to take account of goddesses as well as gods, and where goddess worship was deeply rooted, it was inevitable that there should occur combinations of sex. This actually took place in the worship of Mithra. Herodotus, writing in the fifth century B.C., affirms that in some way Mithra was identified with a goddess. Referring to the Persians he says: "It is not their practice to erect statues or temples or altars, but they charge those with folly who do so; because, as I conjecture, they do not think the gods have human forms as the Greeks do. They are accustomed to ascend the highest parts of the mountains and offer sacrifice to Zeus, and they call the whole circle of the heavens by the name Zeus. They sacrifice to the sun and moon, to the earth, fire, water and the winds. To these alone they have sacrificed from earliest times, but they have since learnt from the Arabians and Assyrians to sacrifice to Aphrodite (Urania) whom the Assyrians call Mylitta, the Arabians Alitta, and the Persians Mitra." (Bk. 1, c.131.)

This is one of the seemingly improbable statements in Herodotus which research has partly confirmed. He has been accused of blundering in combining Mithra with Mylitta, since monuments show that the Goddess identified with Mithra was Anaitis or Tanat. But it seems clear that the Armenian Anaitis and Mylitta were regarded as the same deity; and there are other clues.

Strabo twice brackets Anaitis with the Persian god Omanus. There is reason to suppose that Omanus was a name of Mithra, derived from Vohu-mano, meaning Good Mind. In any case the fact of the combination of Mithra with a Goddess in a double personality is shown by innumerable monuments and a statement of the fourth century Christian controversialist, Julius Firmicus, and later writers. The double-sexed character is evident in the monument in the British Museum in which the divine slayer of the bull presents a face of perfect and sexless beauty, feminine in its delicate loveliness of feature, with a masculine body. The combination shows the influence of the old Akkado-Babylonian system on the later Mazdean. From the old Akkadians the Semites received the conception of a trinity, the divine father and mother by the side of their son the Sun-god. They tended to give every God a colorless double or wife, and in the final blending of these in a double-sexed deity we have the consummation of the idea. It was not special to Asia. The Egyptians gave a double sex to moon, earth, air, fire and water. The earth was male as rock, female as arable soil; fire was masculine as heat, female as light, and so on. The Greeks and Romans accepted the notion, but it was probably from Chaldea that it reached the Mithraists.

The existence of so many Mithraic monuments points to the disappearance of the old Persian aversion to images of deity. As the faith spread, it assimilated all manner of ancient symbolism and ritual. Mithra is associated with strange, lion-headed, serpentine figures bearing two keys, but above all he is depicted as the slayer of the bull. There are many explanations of the latter. The bull has been variously regarded as a symbol of the earth, the moon, the sun, lust, evil, and the cosmogonic bull of the Magian system. The origin of the symbolism goes back to an ancient Assyrian cult which produced monuments of a divine or kingly personage slaying a lion or a bull by thrusting a sword through him. There can be little doubt that these successive religious representations rest partly on a zodiacal system of sacred symbolism in which the slaying of a given animal means either the passing of the sun into or out of a particular sign of the zodiac at a particular season of the year, or the slaying of the animal represented as a special sacrifice or both.

The zodiac is of immense antiquity. Although the signs no

longer do so, once they must have coincided with the actual constellations whose names they bear. The view that the slaying of the Bull originally pointed to the sun's entering the sign of the Bull either at the vernal equinox or winter solstice is supported by the fact that the bull was once a symbol of the Sun-god and of agriculture, early ploughs being drawn by bulls or oxen. The slaying of the lion would signify the sun's entry into Leo at midsummer and may connect with the worship of Tammuz after whom the midsummer month was named in Syria—unless the God took his name from the month. Owing to the precession of the equinoxes, the constellation Taurus ceased to be the sun's place at the vernal equinox for about 2100 years before the reign of Augustus. Its position was occupied by the constellation of the Ram. But just as the symbol of slaying the lion held its ground after the bull played a similar part, so the sign of the Bull continued to be used after the sun had begun to enter the constellation Aries at the sacred season. During the Christian era the bull was prominent in Mithraic monuments, but there was an actual ceremony of slaying a ram in honor of the Sun-god. In Persia the sign Aries, the Ram, was known as the Lamb; and in some of the Mithraic mysteries during the Christian era it was a lamb that was slain.

Further support for the zodiacal explanation of religious symbols is provided by the ancient worship of a Fish-god. The early Christians called Jesus Christ the Fish. In the zodiac the sign of the Fishes, Pisces, comes next to the Ram; the Fishes had actually taken the place of the Ram at the spring festival when this symbol came into use.

Like every widespread religion, Mithraism is a complex of many ideas. In its Western evolution it became closely associated with the popular worship of Cybele, the Mother of the Gods, and in virtue of Roman military tradition it was linked specifically with Roman deities. In its cave temples, images and names have been found of Juno, Minerva, Apollo, Mars, Bacchus, Mercury and Venus, but more especially Sylvanus, the Latin equivalent of the Greek Pan, who had taken on a pantheistic character. The association of the Sun-god with the Goat-god is often found in Greek mythology and can be traced back to the

Babylonian system on which Mithraism had independently drawn.

Whatever the original significance of slaying the bull, it came to be associated with the idea of sacrifice and purification. The great vogue of the Phrygian institutions of the Taurobolium and Criobolium, or purification by the blood of bulls and rams, must have reacted on Mithraism even if it were not strictly of Mithraic origin. Mithra, like Osiris and Dionysus, was the bull as well as the God to whom the bull was sacrificed, just as Amun, to whom rams were sacrificed, was "the Great ram." In the procedure of the Taurobolia and Criobolia, which became very popular in the Roman world, we have the literal and original meaning of the phrase "washed in the blood of the lamb." The doctrine was that resurrection and eternal life were secured by drenching or sprinkling with the actual blood of a sacrificial bull or ram, often, doubtless a lamb. Thus we have such mortuary inscriptions as *Taurobolio criobolioque in aeternum renatus* (By the bull-sacrifice and the ram-sacrifice born again for eternity). At first the initiate was placed in a pit over which there was a grating. On this was placed the animal to be slain and the blood dropped on the votary beneath. But as there is a constant tendency in mystical systems to substitute symbolism for concrete usages, we may surmise that ultimately the Mithraists performed their sacrificial rites in a less crude form.

THE GOD OF THE CAVE

One peculiarity of the worship of Mithra is that it was carried on in caves. This was considered so important that where natural caves did not exist the devotees made artificial ones. The practice may have its roots in very early times when the Romans threw specimens of all domestic utensils and a handful of Roman earth into a sacred cave on the Palatine Hill. As this was named *mundus* it recalls the belief that Zoroaster consecrated a cave in honor of Mithra, the Maker and Father of all things. The cave was said to be an image of the wrold, which was made by Mithra, and all its contents were symbols of the mundane elements and climate.

A cave seems to have been the earliest form of temple. It is easy to understand that fire- or sun-worshippers, who found in caves the remains of fires of earlier men, may have supposed that the sun himself went into some cave when he passed below the horizon at night. Porphyry tells us that caves in the earliest times were consecrated to the Gods before temples were built. Thus the Curetes in Crete dedicated a cavern to Zeus; in Arcadia a cave was sacred to the moon and to Lycean Pan, and in Naxos to Dionysus. But wherever Mithra was known, he adds, they propitiated him in a cavern.

Mithra was named "rock-born" and a common formula in the cult was "God out of the rock." Many Mithraic altars are cut in the rocks. In these sacred caves the rising sun was hailed with joy, while at night, when the sun was hidden, special prayers would be offered. From time immemorial the first day of the week, Sunday, was consecrated to Mithra, the Sun-god. Sunday was pre-eminently the Lord's Day long before Christianity.

We have some exact information about the two chief Mithraic festivals of the winter solstice, the birthday of the Sun-god, and the vernal equinox, the period of his sacrifice and triumph. It is no longer denied by Christian scholars that Christmas is a solar festival of unknown antiquity, which the early Christians appropriated to their Christ in total ignorance of the real time of his birth. But it is not so freely recognized that Easter is also a solar, or more strictly, a luni-solar festival. Mithra and Osiris, like so many other solar and vegetal deities, were especially adored at the vernal equinox with ceremonies of the symbolical death of the deity, the search for his body, and the finding of it.

Firmicus in his *De Errore* describes how the worshippers laid a stone image at night on a bier and liturgically mourned for it. This symbolic body of the dead God was then placed in the tomb and after a time it was withdrawn, whereupon the worshippers rejoiced and exhorted one another to be of good hope. Lights were brought in and the priest anointed the throats of the devotees, murmuring slowly, "Be of good courage, ye have been instructed in the mysteries and ye shall have salvation from your sorrows." As the stone image in a Mithraic ceremony would be laid in a rock-tomb—Mithra being preeminently "from the rock" and worshipped in a cave—the parallel to the central episode of the Christian story is striking. In view of the duplication of the motive in the cults of Osiris, Attis, Dionysus, it is impossible to doubt that we are dealing with a universal myth.

Frazer has argued that the God who dies and rises again is a Vegetation-god. This may be the case to some extent in the cults of Attis, Adonis, Dionysus and Osiris. On the other hand the solar Heracles dies on the funeral pyre, descends to Hades and reascends to Heaven. The strictly solar Apollo descended into Hades, as did Orpheus. For mortals the descent into Hades is simply death, but since a God cannot cease to exist, he may as well be said to "die" in one way as another. In all these cases, however, the explanation is astronomical, and it was so in the account of Mithra's descent into Hades.

This was only one of the Mithraic mysteries. Another was enacted when a new worshipper was initiated, and probably repeated frequently. Justin Martyr, after describing the institution of the Lord's Supper, as narrated in the gospels, goes on to say: "Which the wicked devils have imitated in the mysteries of Mithra, commanding the same thing to be done. For, that bread and a cup of water are placed with certain incantations in the mystic rites of one who is being initiated, you either know or can learn." Tertullian bears this out. "The devil," he says, "by the mysteries of his idols; imitates even the main parts of the divine mysteries. He also baptizes his worshippers in water and makes them believe that this purifies them of their crimes. . . . There Mithra sets his mark on the forehead of his soldiers; he celebrates the oblation of bread; he offers an image of the resurrection, and presents at once the crown and the sword; he limits his chief priest to a single marriage: he even has his virgins and his ascetics." Again, "the devil has gone about to apply to the worship of idols those very things in which consists the administration of Christ's sacraments."

On Mithraic monuments we find representations of twelve episodes, probably corresponding to the twelve labors in the stories of Heracles, Samson and other Sun-heroes, and probably also connected with initiation. We know that the complete initiation of a worshipper was an elaborate and even painful process. From Porphyry and Jerome we learn that the devotees were divided into a number of different degrees, symbolically marked by the names of animals, the skins and heads of which were sometimes worn. Jerome speaks of gryphon, crow, soldier, lion, Persian (sun), Bromios (or the bull) and father. The list is grotesque, but it is an old story—all religions are absurd to those who do not believe them.

The mark on the forehead of the initiate was in all likelihood the cross, the universal symbol of life and immortality, and in particular of the Sun-god. Presumably it was not the gammadion or swastika, the most specific symbol of the Sun, for that appears to have been absent from Persian art. We may infer that it was one of the normal forms of the Christian cross from the mode of Tertullian's statement and the fact that the *tan* or cross was a forehead mark in the Judaic cult set forth in the Book of Revelations. The symbol entered into the fire-worship of Persia by way of architecture, and it could not have been absent from the imagery of an Eastern Sun-god of the time.

Chapter Eleven

MITHRAISM AND CHRISTIANITY

We have thus far briefly examined what may for the most part be termed the skeleton or dry bones of the Mithraic religion at the period when it seemed to be successfully competing with Christianity. What of the inner life, the spiritual message and attraction which there must have been to give the cult its hold over the Roman Empire? Here it is that our ignorance becomes most sharply felt. So far as Christian zeal could suppress all good report of Mithraism, this was done when Christianity, I will not say overthrew, but absorbed the Mithraic movement. There were in antiquity, we know from Porphyry, several elaborate treatises setting forth the religion of Mithra; and every one of these has been destroyed by the care of the Church. They doubtless included much narrative as well as much didactic matter, the knowledge of which would color the whole religious consciousness of Mithra's worshippers.

We shall see later that clues still exist, one of which has been overlooked in studies of Mithraism, to some of the myths of the cult, and we may safely decide in general that just as the Brahmanas prove the currency of Vedic hymns, so there must have existed a Mithraic mythology which is not contained in the Zendavesta. The reconstruction of that mythology, however, is now hopeless. Too little attention, perhaps, has been paid to Creuzer's theory that the name Perseus-Perses, "the Persian;" and that the Perseus myth is really an early adaptation of the Mithra myth. The story of Perseus certainly has an amount of action and color unusual in Greek myth, and is no less suggestive or Oriental origin than the legend of Heracles. But unless new evidence is forthcoming, such a hypothesis can at most stand for a possibility.

And so with the didactic side of Mithraism, we must limit our inferences to our positive data. These include the evidence of the Venidad ritual that there was associated with the cult a teaching of happy immortality for the righteous, very much on the lines of that of Christianity. An extract will make the point clear:

"(Zarathustra asked) O Maker of the material world, thou Holy One! Where are the rewards given? Where does the rewarding take place? Where is the recompense fulfilled? Whereto do men come to take the reward that, during their life in the material world, they have won for their souls?

"Ahura Mazda answered: When the man is dead, when his time is past, then the wicked, evil-doing Devas cut off his eyesight. On the third night, when the dawn appears and brightens, when Mithra the God with beautiful weapons, reaches the all-happy mountains, and the sun is rising:

"Then the fiend, named Vizaresha, O Spitama Zarathustra, carries off in bonds the souls of the wicked Deva-worshippers who live in sin. The soul enters the way made by Time, and open both to the wicked and to the righteous. At the end of the Kinvad bridge, the holy bridge made by the Mazda, they ask for their spirits and souls the reward for the worldly goods which they gave away here below.

"Then comes the beautiful, well-shapen, strong and graceful maid, with the dogs at her sides, one who can discern, who has many children, happy and of high understanding. She makes the soul of the righteous one go up above the Haraberezaiti; above the Kinvad bridge; she places it in the presence of the heavenly Gods themselves.

"Uprises Vohu-mano from his golden seat; Vohu-mano exclaims: How hast thou come to us, thou Holy One, from that decaying world into this decaying one?

"Gladly pass the souls of the righteous to the golden seat of Ahura-Mazda, to the golden seat of Amesha-Spentas, to the Garoumanem (house of songs) the abode of Ahura-Mazda, the abode of Amesha-Spentas, the abode of all the other holy beings.

"As to the godly man that has been cleansed, the wicked evil-doing Devas tremble at the perfume of his soul after death, as doth a sheep on which a wolf is pouncing.

"The souls of the righteous are gathered together there: Nairyo-Sangha is with them: a messenger of Ahura-Mazda is Nairyo-Sangha."

It is noteworthy, further, that in some codices of the Avesta is found this formula: "He has gained nothing who has not gained the soul: He shall gain nothing who shall not gain the soul." The meaning is "gain a place in Paradise," and the passage looks very much like an original form of a well-known Christian text.

UNFOUNDED CHARGES

For the rest, the Zendavesta, like most other sacred books, insists on the normal morals strenuously enough. It has strange special teachings as to the sacrosanctity of the dog, and its veto alike on the burning and the burying of bodies is peculiar to Mazdeism. But these beliefs do not seem to have affected later Mithraism; whereas probably its special stress on truthfulness was maintained. We cannot, indeed, tell how the Mithraic priests dealt with the special problems of the life of the Roman Empire, but we are entitled, none the less, to protest against the loose revival of unfounded and exploded charges against the cult.

To this day we find Christian scholars either saying or hinting that Mithraism was signalized in the Roman period by human sacrifices. For this there is no justification. The ecclesiastical historian Socrates does indeed allege that about the year 360 a temple of Mithra at Alexandria, long empty and neglected, was granted by Constantine to the Christians; that they found in it an *adytum* of vast depth, containing the skulls of many persons, old and young, who had been sacrificed to Mithra, and that the Christians paraded them through the city, whereupon there was a riot in which Bishop George and many others were slain. But this narrative is unsupported even in ecclesiastical history, and is full of incredibilities.

The "Pagans" in general are represented as taking arms to avenge an attack on the Mithraic sect, though the Mithraic temple is expressly declared to have been long deserted, and the emperor Julian, a Mithraist, is represented as writing a letter denouncing the Alexandrians for their conduct. Yet he merely speaks of the killing of George, whereas Socrates alleges a wholesale massacre. The whole story savors of mere *odium theologicum*, and will not fit with any other accounts of Mithraic worship. We do know that during the whole of the first three or four centuries it was charged against the Christians, by Jews or Pagans, that they were wont to sacrifice a child at their mysteries. That charge was doubtless false, but it was constantly made.

On the other hand, the only kind of record founded on for the charge against Mithraism is one which rebuts it. Sainte-Croix, in his "Recherches" (ii. 135), referred to a passage in Lampridius's life of Commodus in which he is said to have "*polluted* the rites of Mithras *by a real homicide*, where it is usual for something to be said or done for the purpose of causing terror." The same scholar makes another reference which equally serves to confute him; yet an English writer later speaks of "the dark and fearful mysteries" of Mithra. That assertion also is plainly valueless, coming as it does from a Christian writer of the tenth century, and being absolutely without ancient corroboration. What seems to have happened was a symbolical sacrifice, perhaps followed up by a symbolic eating of the God's image—proceedings which, there is good reason to suppose, occurred in the mysteries of the early Christians.

But there is far more testimony, such as it is, for the charge of infamous procedure against the Christians than against the Mithraists. The Mithraic mysteries, save for the fact that they involved real austerities and a scenic representation of death, were no more dark and fearful than the Christian mysteries are known to have been, not to speak of what these are *said* to have been. There lies against them no such imputation of licence as was constantly brought against the midnight meetings of the Christians, or as is specifically brought by Paul against his own converts at Corinth. Their purpose was unquestionably moral as well as consolatory. In the words of Suidas, the worshipper went through his trials in order that he should become holy and passionless. In the course of the initiation—as we know from the unwilling admiration of Tertullian—the devotee, called the soldier of Mithra, was offered a crown, which it was his part to refuse, saying that Mithra was his crown. And everything points to the enunciation of a theory of expiation of and purification from sin, in which Mithra figured as Mediator and Savior, actually undergoing a symbolic sacrifice, and certainly securing to his worshippers eternal life.

As to the doctrine of immortality being pre-Christian, the whole Mithraic symbolism implies such a teaching. On most of the bull monuments, it will be remembered, there stand beside Mithra two figures, one holding a raised and one a lowered torch. These signified primarily sunrise and sunset, or rising spring sun and sinking autumn sun, but they were also the ancient symbols for life and death, and would further signify the fall and return of the soul.

Nor was this the only point at which Mithraism is known to have competed with Christianity in what pass for its highest attractions. The doctrine of the *Logos*, the Incarnate Word or Reason, which Christianity absorbed through the Platonizing Jews of Alexandria, was present in Mithraism, and of prior derivation. That Mithra was connected with "the Word" appears from the Avesta. In the Venidad, further, Zarathustra is made to praise successively Mithra "of the most glorious weapons," Sraosha, "the Holy One," and "the Holy Word, the most glorious," thus joining and in part identifying Mithra with the Word as well as joining him with the Holy Spirit. And Emanuel Deutsch was of opinion that the Metatron of the Talmud (whom he equates with the Ideas of Plato, the *Logos* of Philo, the "Word of Aziluth" of the Kabbalists, the *Sophia* or Power of the Gnostics and the *Nous* of Plotinus) was "most probably nothing but Mithra." As the Metatron is on the Jewish side identified with the "Angel" promised as leader and commander to the Hebrews in Palestine, and that angel is quasi-historically represented by Joshua-Jesus, the chain of allusion from Mithra to the Christ is thus curiously complete.

There seems no good reason for supposing that the doctrines of the *Logos* and the Trinity reached the Persians through the Greeks; on the contrary, they probably acquired them from Babylonian sources, on which the Greeks also drew; and it was not improbably their version of the *Logos* idea that gave the lead to the Philonic and Christian form, in which the Word is explicitly "the light of the world."

Of course, we are told that the Mithraic rites and mysteries were borrowed and imitated from Christianity. The refutation of this notion lies in the language of those Christian fathers who spoke of Mithraism. Three of them, as we have seen, speak of Mithraic resemblances to Christian rites as being the work of devils. Now, if the Mithraists *had* simply imitated the historic Christians, the obvious course for the latter would be simply to say so. But Justin Martyr expressly argues that the demons *anticipated* the Christian mysteries and prepared parodies of them beforehand. "When I hear," he says, "that Perseus was begotten of a virgin, I understand that the deceiving serpent counterfeited also this." Nobody now pretends that the Perseus myth, or the Pagan virgin myth in general, is later than Christianity. Justin Martyr, indeed, is perhaps the most foolish of the Christian fathers, but what he says about the anticipatory action of the demon or demons plainly underlies the argumentation also of Tertullian and Julius Firmicus.

THE ROCK-BORN GOD

When, again, Justin asserts that the Mithraists in their initiation *imitate* not only Daniel's utterance "that a stone without hands was cut out of a mountain," but "the whole of [Isaiah's] words" (Isa.: xxxiii, 13–19), he merely helps us to realize how much older than Christianity is that particular element of Christian symbolism which connects alike Jesus and Peter with the mystic Rock. That Mazdeism or Mithraism borrowed this symbol from Judaism, where it is either an excrescence or a totemistic survival, is as unlikely as it is likely that the Hebrews borrowed it from Babylonia or Persia. In Polynesian mythology—as also in the rites of human sacrifice—where there are so many close coincidences with Asiatic ideas, it was told that the God Taaroa "embraced a rock, the imagined foundation of all things, which afterwards brought forth the earth and sea." Here again we are in touch with the Graecized but probably Semitic myth of the rock-born Agdestis, son of Jupiter.

Even the remarkable parallel between the myth of Moses striking the rock for water and a scene on one of the Mithraic monuments suggests rather a common source for both myths than a Persian borrowing from the Bible. In the monument, Mithra shoots an arrow at a rock, and water gushes forth where the arrow strikes. As the story of the babe Moses is found long before in that of Sargon, so probably does the rock story come from Central Asia.

The passage in Isaiah, which strongly suggests the Mithraic initiation, seems to have been tampered with by the Jewish scribes; and corruption is similarly suspected in the passage Gen.: xlix, 24, where "the Shepherd, the Stone of Israel," points to some belief latterly thrust out of Judaism. Above all, the so-called Song of Moses (in which Israel and his enemies figure as putting their faith in a divine "Rock" and the hostile "Rock" is associated with a wine sacrament) points to the presence of such a God-symbol in Hebrew religion long before our era.

There is a clear Mazdean element, finally, in the allusion to the mystic stone in Zechariah, the "seven eyes" being certainly connected with the Seven Amesha-Spentas, of whom Mithra on one view, and Ormazd on another, was chief. And when we find in the epistles phrases as to Jesus being a "living stone" and a "spiritual rock," and read in the gospels how Jesus said, "Thou art Peter, and upon this rock I will build my church," we turn from the latter utterance, so obviously unhistorical, back to the Mithraic rite. We see in the mystic rock of Mithra, the rock from which the God comes—be it the earth or the cloud—the probable source alike of the Roman legend and the doctrine of the pseudo-Petrine and Pauline epistles.

The Mithraic mysteries, then, of the burial and resurrection of the Lord, the Mediator, and Savior (buried in a rock tomb and resurrected from that tomb), the sacrament of bread and water, the marking on the forehead with a mystic mark—all these were in practice, as were the Egyptian search for the lost corpse of Osiris, and the representation of his entombment and resurrection, before the publication of the Christian Gospel of a Lord who was buried in a rock tomb, and rose from that tomb on the day of the sun, and before the Christian mystery of the Divine communion, with bread and water or bread and wine, which last were before employed also in the mysteries of Dionysus, Sun-God and Wine-God, doubtless as representing *his* body and blood. But even the eucharist of bread and wine, as well as a bread-and-meat banquet, was inferribly present in the Mithraic cultus, for the Zoroastrian Hom or Haoma, identical with the Vedic Soma, was a species of liquor, and figured largely in the old cult as *in itself a sacred thing*, and ultimately as a deity. Indeed, this deification of a drink is held to be the true origin of the God Dionysus, even as Agni is a deification of the sacrificial fire. And whereas the Mazdean lore associated the Haoma-Tree with the Tree of Life in Paradise, so do we find the Catholic theologians making that predication concerning the Christian eucharist.

The "cup" of Mithra had in itself a mystical significance. In the monuments we see drinking from it the sacred serpent, the symbol of wisdom and healing. Again, as there is record of an actual eating of a lamb in early Christian mysteries—a detail still partly preserved in the Italian usage of blessing both a lamb and the baked figure of a lamb at the Easter season, but officially superseded by the wafer of the Mass—so in the Persian cult, the sacrificed flesh was mixed with bread and baked in a round cake called *Myazd* or *Myazda* and sacramentally eaten by the worshippers.

Nor was this all. Firmicus informs us that the devil, in order to leave nothing undone for the destruction of souls, had beforehand resorted to deceptive imitations of the cross of Christ. Not only did they in Phrygia fix the image of a young man to a tree in the worship of the Mother of the Gods, and in other cults imitate the crucifixion in similar ways, but in one mystery in particular the Pagans were wont to consecrate a tree and, towards midnight, to slay a ram at the foot of it. This cult may or may not have been the Mithraic, but there is a strong presumption that Mithraism included such a rite. We have seen that a ram-lamb was sacrificed in the Mithraic mysteries, and not only are there sacred trees on all the typical Mithraic monuments, but the God himself is represented as being reborn or placed within a tree. This is directly assimilated from Osiris, Dionysus and Adonis, and points to the origins of the Christian Holy Cross myth.

AGNUS DEI

The Christian assimilation of Mithraism is, however, still more clearly seen in the familiar Christian symbol in which Christ is represented as a lamb or ram, carrying by one forefoot a cross. We know from Porphyry that in the mysteries a place near the equinoctial circle was assigned to Mithra as an appropriate seat, and on this account he bears the sword of the Ram [Aries] which is a sign of Mars [Ares]. The sword of the Ram, we may take it, was simply figured as the cross, since a sword is a cross.

Again, as we have seen, Porphyry explains that "Mithra is the Bull Demiurgos and lord of generation." Here then would be, as we have already seen, a symbolical slaying, in which the deity is sacrificed by the deity, and we may fairly infer that the symbolic ram in turn would be sacrificed by the Mithraists on the same principle. Now, it appears to be, as we have said, the historic fact that among the early Christians a ram or lamb was sacrificed in the paschal mystery. It is disputed between Greeks and Latins whether at one time the slain lamb was offered on the altar, together with the mystical body of Christ; but it is admitted by Catholic writers—and this, by the way, is the origin of a certain dispute about singing the *Agnus Dei* in church —that in the old *Ordo Ramanus* a lamb was consecrated, slain and eaten, on Easter Day, by way of a religious rite. Of this lamb, too, the blood was received in a cup. Thus everything goes to show not only that the Lamb in the early Christian cultus was a God-symbol from remote antiquity, but that it was regarded in exactly the same way as the symbolical lamb in the Mithraic cult.

In the Apocalypse, one of the earliest quasi-Christian documents, and one that exhibits to us the stage in which Jesuism and the Lamb-God-symbol were still held parts of Judaism, the Gentile differentiation being repudiated, we have the slain Lamb-God described as having seven horns and seven eyes, "which are the seven spirits of God, sent forth unto all the earth," and as holding in his right hand seven stars—that is to say, the seven planetary Mazdean "Amshaspands" or Amesha-Spentas, before mentioned, of which Mithra was the chief and, as it were, the embodiment.

Still further does the parallel hold. It is well known that whereas in the gospels Jesus is said to have been born in an inn stable, early Christian writers, as Justin Martyr and Origen, explicitly say he was born in a cave. Now, in the Mithra myth, Mithra is both rock-born and born in a cave, and the monuments show the newborn babe adored by shepherds who offer first-fruits. And it is remarkable that whereas a cave long was (and I believe is) shown as the birthplace of Jesus at Bethlehem, Saint Jerome actually complained that in his day the Pagans celebrated the worship of Tammuz (%Adonis) and presumably, therefore, the festival of the birth of the sun, Christmas Day, at that very cave.

Given these identities, it was inevitable that, whether or not Mithra was—originally or in the older Mazdean creed—regarded as born of a virgin, he should in his Western cultus come to be so regarded. As we saw, there was a primary tendency, Aryan as well as Semitic, to make the young God the son of the Supreme God, like Dionysus, like Apollo, like Heracles; and when Mithra became specially identified, like Dionysus, with the Phrygian God Sabazios, who was the "child as it were of the [great] Mother," he necessarily came to hold the same relation to the Mother-goddess. But in all likelihood there were ancient Persian forms of the conception to start from. It seems highly probable that the birth-legend of the Persian Cyrus was akin to or connected with the myth of Mithra, Cyrus (Koresh) being a name of the sun, and the legend being obviously solar. Thus it would tend to be told of Mithra that he was born under difficulties, like the other Sun-gods, and his being cave-born would make it the more easy.

It was further practically a matter of course that his mother should be styled a virgin, the precedents being uniform. In Phrygia the God Acdestis or Agdistis, a variant of Attis, associated with Attis and Mithra in the worship of the Great Mother, is rock-born. Like Mithra he is two-sexed, figuring in some versions as a female; and the coarse Greek story of the manner of his birth is evidently a myth framed to account for an epithet. Further, the Goddess Anahita or Anaitis, with whom Mithra was anciently paired, was pre-eminently a Goddess of fruitfulness, and as such would necessarily figure in her cultus as a Mother. As Mithra never appears (save in worshipful metaphors) as a father, he would perforce rank as her son. Precisely so does Attis in the Orphic theosophy figure as the son of Athene, the Virgin Goddess who in turn is possibly a variant of Anaitis and Tanith. Finally, as the pre-eminent spirit Sraosha (-Vohumano) was connected with Mithra, so would there be a blending or assimilation of Mithra with Saoshyas or Saoshyant, the Savior and Raiser of the Dead, who in the Parsee mythology is to be virgin-born, his mother miraculously conceiving him from the seed of Zarathustra.

As a result of all these myth motives, we find Mithra figuring in the Christian empire in the fourth and fifth centuries, alongside of the Christ, as supernaturally born of a Virgin-mother—a mortal maiden or a Mother-goddess—and of the Most High God. If the Christians made much of some occult thesis that Mithra was his own father, or otherwise the spouse of his mother, they were but keeping record of the fact that in this as in so many ancient cults, and more obscurely in their own, the God had been variously conceived as the Son and as the lover of the Mother-goddess. In all probability they took from Mithraism the immemorial ritual of the birth of the Child-god, for in the Mithraic monument we have the figure of the tree overshadowing the newborn child, even as it does in the early Christian sculptures.

Chapter Twelve

THE TRANSFORMATION OF MITHRA

In view of the long series of parallels between the Mithraic and the Christian cults, it is difficult to doubt that one has imitated the other, and it may now be left to the candid reader to pass his own judgment on the theory that it was Mithraism which copied Christism. The Christian imitation took place, be it observed, because the features imitated were found by experience to be religiously attractive, Mithraism itself having, as we have seen, developed some of them on the lines of other Oriental cults. Its history, as far as we can trace it, is a series of adaptations to its environment. Mithraism in fact had spread in the West with just such rapidity as Christians have been wont to count miraculous in the case of their own creed. And we, looking back on Christian and other religious history with sociological eyes, can perfectly understand how such a cultus, with an elaborate ceremonial and an impressive initiation, with the attraction of august and solemn mysteries and the promise of immortal life, and with official encouragement as regards the army, could spread throughout the Roman Empire in the age in which the primitive Roman religion crumbled away before the advance of far more highly specialized and complicated systems and a more philosophic outlook.

So special was the favor accorded to it in Rome that a Mithraeum was permitted to be dug in the Capitoline Hill under the Capitol, the most venerated spot in the city. Above all it was popular in the army, which really seems to have been to some extent a school, albeit a savage one, of moral strength and order at a time when an appalling abjection was overtaking the Roman world, men reverencing rank as dogs reverence men.

One of the first stages in the initiation, for men, consisted in the devotee's receiving a sword, and being called a soldier of Mithra. Hence the association of Mithra with Mars, and his virtual absorption of Janus, whose attributes he duplicated. Thus Mithraism was specially the faith of soldiers, and in doing honor to the Invincible Sun-god Mithra. *Deo Soli Invicto Mithrae*, as the monuments have it, the Emperor Constantine vied with the most loyal Mithraists long after his conversion to Christianity.

The explanation of this phase seems to be that it was through oriental militarism that the cult reached the west. We have it from Plutarch that Mithraism was first introduced to Rome through the Cilician pirates whom Pompey put down, and it is known that those pirates were a confederation of soldiers and others formerly employed by Asian rulers (in particular by Mithradates, in whose army Mithraism would be the natural cult) and thrown on their own resources by the Roman conquest. As such piracy was not reckoned discreditable, and Pompey took many of the defeated pirates under his patronage, their religion had a good start with the Roman army, in which so many of them entered, and which was for centuries afterwards so largely recruited from the East. It is very likely that the Roman authorities from the first encouraged the cult as specially fitted for the soldiery. But the cult was not confined to them.

ABSENCE OF WOMEN

Among the non-military congregations, we learn from the inscriptions, there were both slaves and freedmen, so that the cult was on that side as receptive as the Christian. But in one other respect it seems to have been less so. Among all the hundreds of recovered inscriptions there is no mention of a priestess or woman initiate, or even of a donatress, though there are dedications *pro salute* of women, and one inscription telling of a Mithraeum erected by the priest and his family. It would seem then that, despite the allusion of Tertullian to the "virgins" of

Mithra, women held no recognized place in the main body of the membership. It would seem, indeed, that inasmuch as the cult was conjoined in the West with that of the Great Mother, Cybele, as in the East with that of Anaitis, women must have been associated with it, but if they were apart from the Mithraists proper the latter would be to that extent socially disadvantaged in their competition with Christianity, however appropriate the worship may have been to the life of the army.

Such an attitude of exclusiveness is probably to be set down in part to the spirit of asceticism which, on Tertullian's testimony, marked the Mithraic cultus as it did the Manichaeans and several of the Christian sects. Of none of the ancients can sexual asceticism be predicated more certainly than of Julian, the most distinguished Mithraist of all; such facts dispose of the Christian attempt to charge upon the rival religion a cultus of sensuality. On a picture of the "banquet of the seven priests" in the Mithraic catacomb there are found phrases of the "Eat and drink, for tomorrow we die" order, and these may stand for an antinomian tendency such as was early associated with Christism, though it is not at all unlikely that they were inscribed in a hostile spirit by the hands of Christian invaders of the Mithraic retreat. However that may be, there is absolutely no evidence that Mithraism ever developed such disorders as ultimately compelled the abolition of the love-feast among the Christians.

The Mithraic standards, in fact, seem to have been the higher, though both cults alike were sustained mainly by the common people, apart from the special military vogue of the older system. A Christian historian has even held it likely that "what won sympathy for the worship of Mithra in Rome was the fundamental ethical thought that the deity is set in constant strife with evil. . . . The pure and chaste God of light, of whom no myth related anything but virtue and strife against evil, won many hearts from sin-stained Olympus. . . . Above all, the most ideal characters in the history of imperial Rome gave their protection to the Mithra worship."

In all probability it was the poorer cult of the two, lacking as it did the benefactions of rich women. It has been inferred, from the special developments of Mithraism among the soldiers and the Syrian traders who followed the camp, that it was primarily, in the West, a religion of the humble, like Christianity, and that like Christianity it only slowly attained wealth. But inasmuch as it never imitated the propagandist and financial methods which the Church took over from the later Judaism of the Dispersion, and always maintained a highly esoteric character, it escaped certain of the lowering forces of the Christist movement. One of these was the practice of systematic almsgiving, which attracted a motley mass of both sexes to the Christian churches. Mutual aid there probably was among the Mithraists, who in their capacity of organized groups were able to own their congregational property, but their different religious outlook and tradition excluded large financial developments.

Now, however, arises the great question: How came such a cultus to die out of the Roman and Byzantine empire after making its way so far and holding its ground so long? The answer to that question has never, I think, been fully given, and is for the most part utterly evaded, though part of it has been suggested often enough. The truth is that Mithraism was not overthrown; it was merely transformed.

It had gone too far to be overthrown; the question was whether it should continue to rival Christianity or be absorbed by it. While Julian lived, Mithraism had every prospect of increased vogue and prestige, for the Emperor expressly adopted it as his own cultus. "To thee," he makes Hermes say to him, "I have given to know Mithras, thy Father. Be it thine to follow his precepts, so that he may be unto thee, all thy life long, an assured harbor and refuge; and, when thou must needs go hence, full of good hope, thou mayest take this God as a propitious guide." It is the very tone and spirit of the cult of the Christ, and as we have seen, the Christian Fathers with almost one consent saw in Mithraism the great rival of their own worship. The spirit of exclusiveness which Christianity had inherited from Judaism—a spirit alien to the older paganism but essential to the building up of an organized and revenue-raising hierarchy in the later Roman Empire—made a struggle between the cults inevitable.

The critical moment in the career alike of Mithraism and of

Christianity was the death of Julian who, though biased in favor of all the older Gods, gave a special adherence to the War-god Mithra. Had Julian triumphed in the East and reigned thirty years, matters might have gone a good deal differently with Christianity. His death, however, was peculiarly disastrous to Mithraism, for he fell at the hands of the Persian foe, the most formidable enemy of the later empire, and Mithra was "the Persian" *par excellence*, and the very God of the Persian host. There can be little doubt that Jovian's instant choice of Christianity as his state creed was in large measure due to this circumstance, and that at such a juncture the soldiery would be disposed to acquiesce, seeking a better omen. Yet, even apart from this, we are not entitled to suppose that Mithraism could ever have become the general faith, save by very systematic and prolonged action on the part of the State, to the end of assimilating its organization with that of the Church.

SURVIVAL OF THE FITTEST

Religions, like organisms and opinions, struggle for survival and the fittest survive. That is to say, those survive which are fittest for the actual environment, not fittest from the point of view of another and higher environment. What, then, was the religion best adapted to populations of the decaying Roman Empire, in which ignorance and mean subjection were slowly corroding alike intelligence and character, leaving the civilized provinces unable to hold their ground against the barbarians? An unwarlike population, for one thing, wants a sympathetic and emotional religion; and here, though Mithraism had many attractions, Christianity had more, having sedulously copied every one of its rivals, and developed special features of its own.

The beautiful and immortal youth of the older sun-worships, Apollo, Mithras, Dionysus, was always soluble into a mysterious abstraction; in the Christian legend the God was humanized in the most literal way, and for the multitude, the concrete deity must needs replace the abstract. The gospels gave a literal story: the Divine Man was a carpenter who ate and drank with the poorest of the poor. So with the miracles. The priesthoods of the older religions often, if not always, explained to the initiated in the mysteries the mystical purport which was symbolized by the concrete myths, and in some early Christian writers, as notably Origen, we find a constant attempt so to explain away concrete miracle and other stories as allegories. But gradually the very idea of allegory died out, and priests as well as people came to take everything literally and concretely, until miracles became everyday occurrences. This was the religion for the Dark Ages, for the new northern peoples which had not gone through the Pagan evolution of cults and symbolisms and mysticisms, but whose own traditional faith was too vague and primitive to hold its ground against the elaborate Christian theology and ritual.

We may say indeed that the preference for such a God as Jesus over such a one as Mithra was in full keeping with the evolution of aesthetic taste in the Christian period. Today some may even find it hard to conceive how the Invincible God of the Sun could ever call forth the love and devotion given to the suffering Christ. As we have seen, Mithra too was a suffering God, slain and rising again, victorious over death. To him went out in due season all the passion of the weeping worship of Adonis, but it is in his supernal and glorious aspect that the monuments persistently present him, and for the decaying ancient world it was still possible to take some joy in the vision of beauty and strength. There must still have been many who wondered, not at the adoration given to the mystically figured Persian, beautiful as Apollo, triumphant as Ares, but at the giving of any similar devotion to the gibbeted Jew, in whose legend were tax-gatherers and lepers, epileptics and men blind from birth, domestic traitors and cowardly disciples.

Ethical teaching there was in Mithraism, and for the Mithraists it would be none the less moving as coming from an eternal conquerer, the type of dominion. But even as the best Mithraic monuments themselves tell of the decline of the great art of Greece, so the art of Christism tells of a hastening dissolution in which aesthetic sense and craftsmanship alike sink to the levels of barbarism. In the spheres of Byzantium and of papal Rome, the sculptured Mithra would yearly meet fewer eyes that looked lovingly on grace and delightedly on beauty; more and more eyes that recoiled pessimistically from comeliness and turned vacantly from allegorical or esoteric symbols.

The more we study the survival of Christianity, the more clearly do we see that, in spite of the stress of ecclesiastical strife over metaphysical dogmas, the hold of the creed over the people was a matter of concrete and narrative appeal to everyday intelligence. Byzantines and barbarians alike were held by literalism, not by the unintelligible; for both the symbol had to become a fetish, and for the Dark Ages the symbol of the cross was much more plausibly appealing than that of the God slaying the zodiacal bull. Other substitutions followed the same law of psychological economy. Thus it was that Christianity turned the mystic rock, *Petra*, first into the Christ, but later into the chief disciple *Petros*; made an actual tunic of the mystic seamless robe of the Osirian and Mazdean mysteries, the symbol of light and sky; caused to be performed at a wedding feast, for the convenience of the harder drinkers among the guests, the Dionysian miracle of turning water into wine; made Jesus walk on the water not merely in poetry and symbol, as did Poseidon, but for the utilitarian purpose of trying Peter's faith and saving him; and put the scourge of Osiris in the Lord's hand for the castigation of those who defiled the temple by unspiritual traffic. There can be little question as to which plane of doctrine was the more popular. The Christian tales, in a different moral climate, represent exactly the commonplace impulse which built up the bulk of Greek mythology by way of narratives that reduced to an anecdotal basis mystic sculptures and mysterious rites.

But that was not all. The fatal weakness of Mithraism, as pitted against Christianity, was that its very organization was esoteric. For, though an esoteric grade is a useful attraction, and was so employed by the Church, a wholly esoteric institution can never take hold of the ignorant masses. Mithraism was always a sort of freemasonry, never a public organization. What the Christians did was to start, like Rome herself, from a republican basis, combining the life elements of the self-supporting religious associations of the Greeks with the connecting organization of the Jewish synagogues, and then to proceed to build up a great organization on the model of that of republican and imperial Rome—an organization so august for an era of twilight that the very tradition of it could serve the later world to live by for a thousand years. The Christian Church renewed the spell of imperial Rome, and brought actual force to make good intellectual weakness. And so we read that the Mithraic worship was by Christian physical force suppressed in Rome and Alexandria, in the year 376 or 377, at a time when, as the inscriptions show, it was making much headway.

At Rome, the deed was done by the order of the Christian prefect Gracchus, but the proceeding was specifically one of ecclesiastical malice, since even so pious an emperor as Gratian dared not decree a direct assault upon an esteemed pagan cult. But, once begun, the movement of destruction spread, and the Church, which still makes capital of the persecution it suffered at pagan hands, outwardly annihilated the rival it could not spiritually defeat.

In an old Armenian history of the reign of Tiridates, it is told how St. Gregory destroyed in the town of Pakaiaridj the temple of Mihr "called the son of Aramazd," took its treasure "for the poor," and consecrated the ground to the Church. But such acts of piratical violence, which had been made easy by the earlier check to Mithraism in its special field, the army, only obscured the actual capitulation made by the Church to the Mithraic as to the other cults which it absorbed. Even the usages which it could not conveniently absorb, and therefore repudiated, prevailed within its own fold for centuries, so that in the eighth century we find Church Councils commanding proselytes no more to pay worship to fanes and rocks. And there were other survivals. But all that was a trifle as compared with the actual survival of Mithraic symbols and rites in the very worship of Christ. As to the sacrifice of the lamb at the end of the seventh century, a general Council ventured to resist the general usage of picturing Christ as a lamb, but the veto was useless; the symbol survived.

MITHRAIC CHRISTIANS

Some Mithraic items went, but more remained. The Christian bishop went through a ceremony of espousing the Church, following the old mystery in which occurred the formula, "Hail to thee, new spouse; hail, new light." His mitre was called a crown, or tiara, which answered to the headdress of Mithra and the Mithraic priests, as to those of the priests of Egypt; he wore red military boots, now said to be "emblematical of that spiritual warfare on which he had entered," in reality borrowed from the military worship of Mithra, perhaps as early as Jovian. And the higher mysteries of communion, divine sacrifice, and resurrection, as we have seen, were as much Mithraic as Christist, so that a Mithraist could turn to the Christian worship and find his main rites unimpaired, lightened only of the burden of initiative austerities, stripped of the old obscure mysticism, and with all things turned to the literal and the concrete, in sympathy with the waning of knowledge and philosophy throughout the world.

The Mithraic Christians actually continued to celebrate Christmas Day as the birthday of the sun, despite the censures of the Pope; and their Sunday had been adopted by the supplanting faith. When they listened to the Roman litany of the holy name of Jesus, they knew they were listening to the very epithets of the Sun-god—God of the skies, purity of the eternal light, king of glory, sun of justice, strong God, father of the ages to come, angel of great counsel. In the epistles of Paul they found Christian didactics tuned to the very key of their mystical militarism.

Their priests had been wont to say that "he of the cap" was "himself a Christian." They knew that "the Good Shepherd" was a name of Apollo; that Mithra, like Hermes and Jesus, carried the lamb on his shoulders; that both were mediators, both creators, both judges of the dead. Like some of their sacred caves, and so many pagan temples, the Christian churches looked toward the east. Their soli-lunar midnight worship was preserved in midnight services, which carried on the purpose of the midnight meetings of the early Christians, who had simply followed Essenian, Egyptian, Asiatic, and Mithraic usage, there being no basis for the orthodox notion that these secret meetings were due to fear of persecution. Their *myazd* or *mizd*, or sacred cake, was preserved in the *mass*, which possibly copied the very name.

Above all, their mystic Rock, Petra, was presented to them in the concrete as the rock Peter, the foundation of the Church.

It has been elsewhere shown that the myth of the traitorous Peter connects with those of Proteus and Janus as well as with that of Mithra, inasmuch as Janus also had "two faces," led the twelve months as Mithra presided over the zodiacal signs and Peter over the twelve apostles and, like Proteus and Peter and the Time-god in the Mithraic cult, bore the heavenly keys. Here again, the mythical development of Peter probably follows on that of Jesus; at all events Jesus, too, has several of the attributes of Proteus-Janus: e.g. "I am the door;" "I stand at the door and knock;" "I am in the Father and the Father in me" (-Janus with the two faces, old and young, seated in the midst of the twelve altars); "I have the keys of death and of Hades." The function of Janus as God of War is also associable with the dictum, "I came not to bring peace but a sword."

Finally, the epiphany is in January. But there is to be noted the further remarkable coincidence that in the Egyptian Book of the Dead Petra is the name of the divine doorkeeper of heaven —a circumstance which suggests an ancient connection between the Egyptian and Asiatic cults. On the other hand, the early Christian sculptures which represent the story of Jesus and Peter and the cock-crowing suggest that it originated as an interpretation of some such sculpture; the frequent presence of the cock, as a symbolic bird of the Sun-god, in Mithraic monuments, raises again a presumption of a Mithraic source. There is even some ground for the view that the legend of St. George is but an adaptation of that of Mithra, and it is not unlikely that St. Michael, who in the Christian East is the bearer of the heavenly keys, is in this aspect an adaptation from the Persian War-god. The dragon-slayer clearly derives from Babylon.

From the Mithraists, too, apparently, came the doctrine of purgatory, nowhere set forth in the New Testament save in the spurious epistle of Peter. And though their supreme symbol of Mithra slaying the bull was perforce set aside, being incapable of assimilation, they knew that the Virgin Mother was but a variant of the Goddess-Mothers whose cults had at various times been combined with those of Mithra, and some of whose very statues served as Madonnas; even as the doctrines of the Logos and the Holy Spirit and the Trinity were borrowed from their own and older Asiatic cults, and those of Egypt.

It has chanced, indeed, that those Christian sects which most fully adopted the theosophies of Paganism have disappeared under the controlling power of the main organization, which, as we have said, held by a necessity of its existence to a concrete and literal system, and for the same reason to a rigidly fixed set of dogmas. We know that the Gnostics adopted Mithra, making his name into a mystic charm from which they got the number 365, as from the mystic name Abraxas. Manichaeism, too, the greatest and most tenacious of all the Christian schisms, carried on its ascetic front the stamp of the Persian environment in which it arose, and visibly stands for a blending of the ascetic and mystic elements of Mithraism and Christianity. For the celebration of the slain Christ it practically substituted that of the slain Manes, at the paschal season, reducing the crucifixion to a mere allegory of the cult of vegetation, and identifying the power and wisdom of the Savior-god with the sun and moon. Neither its adherents nor its opponents avowed that it was thus a fresh variant of Mithraism, but the Mithraists cannot have failed to see and signalize alike the heretical and the orthodox adaptation, and it is clear that Mithraism not only entered into Manichaeism but prepared the way for it in the West—the more reason why Mithras should be tabooed by the organized Church. Thus, then, we can understand why the very name seemed at length to be blotted out. And yet, despite all forcible suppression, not only do the monuments of the faith endure and ceremonies survive as part of the very kernel of the Christian worship, but its record remains unknowingly graven in the legend on the dome of the great Christian temple of Rome, destined to teach to later times a lesson of human history, and of the unity of human religion, more enduring than the sectarian faith that is proclaimed within.

We have already seen how at a variety of points the myth of Peter is a development of that of Jesus, and how, alike as leader of the twelve, fisherman, "rock," and bearer of the keys of heaven and hell, the first disciple assimilates with Mithra and Janus, who severally or jointly had those attributes, and whose join cult acquired a special status in the Roman Empire as being at once that of the army and (on the side of Janus) that of the immemorial city. And whereas the legendary Peter thus closely conformed in symbol to the "God out of the Rock," the chief priest of the Mithraic cult at Rome compared no less closely with the Christian bishop, ultimately distinguished as *Papa*-Father. Among the grades of the Mithraists were that of the *Patres Sacrorum*, or Fathers of the Mysteries, and that of the *Pater Patrum*, Father of the Fathers, whose seat was at Rome; and while there was a sacred Mithraic cave under the Capitol, we know from monumental remains that Mithraic worship was conducted on the Vatican Mount, where also was a temple of the Mother-goddess Cybele, and where also dwelt the *Archi-Gallus*, or archeunuch, the head of the cult of Cybele and Attis.

As the ruling tendency of the later Paganism was to combine or "syndicate" all the leading cults, and as Roman patricians were then wont to hold at once the priesthoods of various Gods, it is not surprising to find that in the year 376, under the Empererors Valens and Valentinian, one Sextilius Agesilaus Aedesius was *Pater Patrum Dei Solis Invicti Mithrae*, "born again for eternity through the *taurobolium* and the *cribolium*," and at the same time priest of Hecate and of Bacchus, as well as an adorer of the Mother of the Gods and Attis. On the Vatican Mount, then, if anywhere, would be the seat of the pagan Pope who looked to the Sun-god as his Savior, and worshipped the Mother of the Gods.

ST. PETER'S CHAIR

It has been unsuspectingly asserted on the Christian side that the pagans raised their later shrines on the Vatican Mount by way of profaning the site of the grave of St. Peter. We are now entitled to conclude that, on the contrary, the grave of St. Peter was located by tradition on the Vatican Mount because that was the Roman site of the pagan cult to which the myth of Peter was specially assimilated. His grave was assigned where his legend was adumbrated, and, it may be, where his chair was found. For there is some reason to suppose that the "chair of St. Peter" is simply the chair of the *Pater Patrum*, the supreme pontiff of Mithra at Rome.

In reality, the "chair of St. Peter" is a somewhat nondescript object, of which the ornamentation does not fully exhibit either the twelve signs of the zodiac or the twelve labors of Heracles. It was exhibited to the public in 1867, photographed, and at that time examined by the eminent archaeologist, de Rossi, who pronounced it to be in part of old oak much worn, containing a number of inlaid panels of carved ivory in the classic style, representing the labors of Hercules. The whole structure, however, had been renewed by supports and cross-pieces of acacia-wood, of which the ornamentation is medieval. In Rossi's opinion the older portions probably formed originally the curial chair of a senator, and it may be that the whole thing is thus a fortuitous importation, like so many other ecclesiastical relics. But there is an obvious possibility that it is a relic of a pre-Christian cult, and this is rather more likely than would be the sanctification of a mere senator's chair.

The ivory panels, eighteen in number, and not easy to decipher in a photograph, answer in part to the labors of Hercules; a few have simply the zodiacal signs from which the legend of the twelve labors was originally framed; some suggest rather the labors of Perseus, and some closely resemble episodes in the Mithraic monuments. It is not impossible, then, that the whole is an ancient artist's combination, for a syncretic cult, of a number of the symbols of oriental sun-worship, to which all three legends belong. The myth of Perseus (perhaps—the Persian) is at bottom identical with that of Heracles, and in Rome the Mithraists would be very ready to bracket the later conquering Sun-god with the older, the more so because their monuments presented scenes of the same order, and conjunction of cults was the fashion of the day.

The old Roman Hercules, it will be remembered, was a quite different deity from the Grecian Heracles, who was a variant of the Semitic Melkarth and Samson, and though that Heracles was worshipped under the later pagan emperors by his Latin name, it does not appear that at Rome his cult was latterly flourishing. Tertullian asserts that in his day there has been seen (vidimus) a man burnt alive as Hercules (—Heracles), but though this was a ritual sacrifice its solitary celebration tells rather of a Roman show than of a cult.

There were two shrines of Hercules Victor on the Capitoline Hill, and some three other *aedes* in other districts, but the inscriptions of the period show no such interest in his cult as in those of Mithra and other eastern deities. There was in fact no ritualistic worship of Hercules or Heracles at Rome; nothing to account for the use of such a chair; whereas the mysteries of Mithra were among the most elaborate in existence, and the Mithraic priesthood one of the most august. Finally, we know from Porphyry, and from the monuments, that Mithra was habitually represented in the midst of the zodiacal circle, so that the pretended Petrine chair is in every way congruous with his worship. The fact that, in the Mithraic monuments, the zodiac begins with Aquarius, who in ancient art is represented somewhat as a fisherman, would of course appeal to the champions of Peter, whose ancient festival at Rome (January 18) coincided with the sun's entering Aquarius in the calendar. It is also historic fact that the Mithraic order of the zodiac, beginning on the right with Aquarius, and ending on the left with Capricorn, was imitated in Christian art.

If, as we have surmised, an official substitution of Christism for Mithraism began under Jovian when the latter cult was discredited for Roman purposes by the defeat and death of Julian at the hands of the Persians, it is likely enough that an official change of the kind was effected at Rome, the Mithraic *Pater* being either superseded or simply Christianized. In taking over the status of the Mithraic pontiff, the Christian *Papa* of Rome would acquire whatever remained of his influence in the army and in the civil service, besides completing the process of uniting in his own person the symbolisms in virtue of which he was head of the visible Church. It was thus in many ways fitting that he should take to himself the actual chair of the *Pater Patrum*. However that may be, the historical and documentary facts enable us to infer broadly the line of adaptation of Mithraism to the Christian cult. It was presumably thus:

1. Before the Gospels were written, Jesus as "Lamb" was assimilated to Mithra in respect (a) of his attributes of "Seven Spirits" and "seven stars;" (b) of his symbol of the Rock; and (c) of the mystic keys borne by the Time-God in his mysteries. In all three cases there seem to have been ancient Judaic myths to proceed upon.

2. The resurrection ritual, with its rock tomb, and the eucharist of bread and wine, may have been equally ancient even in Jewry, but

there is reason to suppose that both were consciously assimilated to the Mithraic mysteries.

3. As the Mithraic *Pater Patrum* assumed the symbols of the God, and the Christian bishop of Rome imitated the *Pater Patrum*, the tradition came to transfer from Jesus to Peter, the reputed founder of the Roman see, the attributes of the Persian God, and of those with whom he was identified in Rome. Thus whereas Jesus had been key-bearer and Rock before the Gospels were current, Peter finally was foisted on the Gospel in both capacities, while the more exclusively divine attribute of headship of the Seven Spirits was practically dropped from Christian doctrine, and even the symbol of the lamb was discountenanced. They had done their work, and were finally both incongruous and inconvenient.

Chapter Thirteen

THE RELIGIONS OF ANCIENT AMERICA

The native religions of North and South America, like the peoples who held them, seem to stand apart from the rest of humanity, unrelated, underived, independent. The first question that occurs to the ethnologist when he looks at the native American races is: How, and when did they get there? We assume a unity in the human race, and decline to believe that different human species were independently evolved from lower forms in different continents.

There are clear traces of the existence of man in the Mississippi valley between fifty and sixty thousand years ago. Paleolithic man may have entered America earlier, in the inter-glacial period, but it seems probable that he came via the Bering Strait or Greenland and Labrador. The first migration was from Asia and was followed by successive waves. The migrants must have brought with them the germs of myth and ritual practices common in Asia, and we should expect to find coincidences between American, Asiatic, European and Polynesian religious systems.

At the Bering Strait, Asia and America are almost in sight of each other, and at one time they were united. And if we suppose a migration of tribes like the Kamtskadals, who easily bear extreme cold being but slightly civilized, we dispose of all such difficulties as the suggestion that pastoral Mongols would never have crossed without some of their animals.

In the nature of the case, the primary separation of the American from the Asiatic races being admittedly very remote, there are not many close parallels to be expected. A number of extraordinary correspondences, however, have been traced, which point to migrations posterior to the Stone Ages. Take that, for instance, between the Aztec calendar signs and the Mongolian zodiac. The symbols in the Mongolian calendar are borrowed from animals. Four of the twelve are the same as the Aztec. Three others are as nearly the same as the different species of animals in the two hemispheres would allow. The remaining five refer to no creature then found in Anahuac. The resemblance went as far as it could.

No less remarkable is the analogy between the Mexican system of reckoning years by cycles and that still in use over a great part of Asia, seeing that this complex arrangement answers no useful purpose, inasmuch as mere counting by numbers, or by signs numbered in regular succession would have been a far better arrangement. Such a correspondence must be allowed to count for much; and there is also a remarkable, though perhaps not a conclusive, resemblance between the Aztec, pre-Aztec, and Peruvian temple-pyramids and those of Mesopotamia which derived from the earlier Akkadians or Sumerians. Ruins of these still exist in Central America and Peru which can be compared with the records of those of Babylonia and the one example at Saqqara in Egypt.

Those temples or "mountain houses" doubtless began as graves, and grew into great mounds of earth, like those found in the Mississippi valley; and the Asiatic like the Mexican pyramid was built of several terraces. Five seems to have been long a common number in Asia, the Babylonian number seven being reached only at a later period; five was the number of stages or stories in the great temple of Huitzilopochtli, the Mexican national God. The fact that such pyramid temples, or tombs of the same type—the former often carefully covered with masonry, and having likewise in some cases five stages—are found in many of the South Sea Islands, gives a fresh reason for supposing an ancient distribution of races eastward from Asia, in repeated waves of migration. So, too, we are entitled to surmise kinship, when we find that the Mexicans and some Redskin tribes had a fixed usage of throwing the first morsels of their meals into the fire. Something like this is the practice of the islanders of Lamotrek in the Carolines and those of Efate in the New Hebrides, and many Tungusian, Mongolian, and Turkish tribes persistently do the same thing to this day. It is difficult to believe that the peculiar usages of sacrificing a "messenger" or "ambassador" to the Sun, painting him red, and hanging up his and other victims' skins, stuffed, as possessing a sacred efficacy, were independently evolved in the two hemispheres.

Even the practice of scalping seems to be peculiar to the Redskins and the kindred Polynesians, and, in a modified form, to the Mongols. The Mexicans, like the ancient Semites and their Sumer-Akkadian teachers, passed their children "through the fire" to the Fire-god. What is more significant is that they had the Semitic custom of making certain of their special sacrificial observances last for five days.

COMMON SYMBOLISM

There are remarkable concrete parallels, also, in the religious practices and symbolism of Asia and Mexico, apart from those which may be taken as universal. Thus a stone or metal mirror was the symbol, and the source of the name, of the Mexican God Tezcatlipoca, and it is also the outstanding symbol in Japanese Shintoism, a very primitive Asiatic cult. It is told, again, of the national God and War-god Huitzilopochtli that, when the people came to Mexico from their homes, his wooden image with certain war-emblems was carried by four priests in an ark or chest, called the Seat of God. Here we have a widespread usage, but it is significant that it is found in some closely similar form among Mongols, Chinese and Japanese.

So with the casting of children's horoscopes. More specific is the parallel between certain Mexican usages and those of the Buddhist priests of Tibet and Japan. Singularly suggestive of Buddhist contacts, however, are a number of Mexican sculptures; many figures of Quetzalcoatl are practically identical with the established type of Buddha, and other carvings show hardly less close parallels. But no less significant of a general Asiatic connection, perhaps, is a circumstance which has not been much considered by the ethnologists, though it has been noted by the anthropologists—the fact, namely, that both in ancient Asia and in ancient America men kept records by means of knots in strings.

The Chinese in old times are known to have done so, and it is told of the Dravidian Khonds of Orissa that when brought to European knowledge sixty years ago they kept all accounts by knots on strings, and conceived of their Gods as recording men's faults in the same fashion. This would seem to be exactly the method of mnemonics used by the Peruvians when they were discovered by the Spaniards, their *quipus* being described in the same terms. There is evidence that the same device was used in Central America, and perhaps among the Tlascalans, though it had gone into disuse among the Mexicans, who had attained to the use of hieroglyphics.

There remains the question of the source and nature of those hieroglyphics. To examine it in detail is beyond the scope of this survey, and it must suffice to say that as the Mexican hieroglyphic system proper represents an early stage in the evolution of writing from pictures to phonetic symbols, with a phonetic system developed alongside of it, the phenomena are quite consistent with the hypothesis of culture influences from Asia at a remote period. It is not necessary to identify glyphs in order to infer that the Chinese, Egyptian and Aztec systems are akin. The Egyptian symbols remained substantially undeveloped for at least two thousand years, and recent specialists are satisfied that many of the elements of hieroglyphic writing had been growing upon the banks of the Nile long before the time of the first historic dynasty. Given such a slow rate of growth, and noting the fact that Mexican and Egyptian hieroglyphics, and Chinese script, are all written in columns, we are provisionally entitled to see in all three the stages of a continuous evolution.

It is true that the American languages, while demonstrably akin to each other, like the Indo-European group, show little or no relation to any of the languages of Asia. But though the difficulty of fully proving affinities of language between American and Asiatic races is great, and we seem thus bound to suppose a very remote separation indeed. On the other hand, the extraordinary difference between the tongues of American Indians of the same race, and the observed facts as to the rapid changes of language among South Sea islanders, when isolated from each other, go to suggest that very wide deviation may occur in a few thousands of years among people of one stock who have separated at a stage in which they have no literature, and only the material beginnings of a ritual.

Beyond this we need not go. It suffices that there is no conceptual obstacle to the assumption that the civilization of pre-Christian America grew from the central Asiatic roots which fed the beginnings of civilization as we know it in Mediterranean Asia and Europe, and that from the practical certainty of an original migration of Asiatics to America there follows the probability that there occurred several more, at different stages of Asiatic evolution. The hypothesis which seems best to meet all the facts is that America was first peopled from Asia at an extremely remote period; that there grew up slowly American races with a certain definite type of language; and that later immigrants from Asia or Polynesia, perhaps coming as conquerors in virtue of importing a higher civilization, were linguistically absorbed in the earlier mass, as conquering invaders have repeatedly been in the known history of Europe.

All this was recognized by the Swiss historian J. G. Muller, whose *Amerikanische Urreligionen* was written when the real unity of the human race was still obscure, in that it was affirmed on such fantastic bases as the myth of an originally created pair. The counter-hypothesis of creation "in nations" and theories of a peopling of America by the "ten lost tribes" were also much in vogue. There need then be no serious dispute over the thesis that the origin of the ancient American religions is to be sought for in the nature of the human spirit—a different thing from saying that they are autochthonous. The true proposition is neither that, as Muller says, the American peoples did *not* receive their religions from the peoples of the Old World, nor that they *did*: both formulas are misleading. Inasmuch as their ancestors were distinctly human when they first passed from Asia to America, the germs of religion and of many rites were derivative, but like all other peoples they evolved in terms of universal law. As their migrations are likely to have occurred in different epochs, and from different stocks, we may look to find in them, scattered as they are over an entire hemisphere, hardly less variations in language, aspects and civilization than were to be traced in the races of the old world a few thousand years ago.

Such variation is actually seen when we seek to ascertain the connection of the different peoples of Ancient America with each other. For among these there is fully as much variation as is found among the peoples of Europe. To go no further, the Aztecs or Mexicans differ noticeably in certain physical characteristics from the Redskins, and these again show considerable variations of type. A decisive theory of the culture-histories of these people cannot yet be constructed, inasmuch as we are still very much in the dark as to the civilizations which existed in Central and South America before those of Mexico and Peru.

EARLIER CIVILIZATIONS

The two religious systems we have chiefly to consider, the Mexican and Peruvian as they existed before the Spanish Conquest, are not very ancient in their developed form because even the two civilizations were comparatively modern. The Aztecs and the Peruvians, as regards to their then situation, professed to date back only a few centuries from the Conquest; and in both Peru and Mexico there were and still are the architectural remains of civilizations, some of which were themselves so ancient as to be unintelligible to the nations found by the Spaniards. Thus, near Lake Titicaca in Peru, there are wonderful remains of structures, which by their size suggest giant builders, the work of a race whom the Incas overthrew. Yet further, there are remains of rude circles of standing stones which belonged to a primitive civilization far more ancient still. So, in Mexico, there are ancient ruins, such as those at Palanque, which suggests a civilization higher, on the side of art and architecture, and at the same time much older than that of the Aztecs.

All we can say with any safety is that the earlier civilizations grew up in those regions where there were combined the conditions of a regular, easy and abundant food supply—namely, heat and moisture, without an overwhelming proportion of the latter, such as occurs in Brazil. Now, from the point of view of the needs of an early civilization, the golden mean occurs, in South America, only in the territories which were covered by the empire of the Incas, and farther north, from the Isthmus of Panama to Mexico. We surmise, then, a long-continued movement of population southwards, one wave pushing on another before it, till some reached Patagonia.

After a time, however, there might be a backflow. It is admitted that Mexican tradition points to early developments of civilization about the Isthmus and Central America, and then waves of migration and conquest northwards. And it may have been that the people called the Toltecs, who flourished in Mexico before the Aztecs, and were in several respects more highly civilized than they, represented yet again a backflow of one of these peoples from the north, according to the tradition. Their silent disappearance, after four centuries of national life, is the standing puzzle of Mexican history. All that we know is that Mexico remained the seat of the most flourishing empires, mainly because it could best yield an abundant and regular supply of vegetable food, such as maize, and that when Cortes invaded it, the civilization of the Aztecs, who constituted the most powerful of the several Mexican States then existing, was among the most remarkable.

And herein lies the instructiveness of these civilizations, with their religions, that they supply us with a set of results practically independent of all the known history of Europe and Asia. It has been remarked that the great drawback of most of the human sciences is that they do not admit of experiments as do the physical sciences. You must take the phenomena you get and try to account for them, with no aid from planned repetitions of cases. But, on the other hand, the human sciences as latterly organized have an enormous wealth of data lying ready at hand, and some collocations of data have for us the effect of new revelations in human affairs.

After men became absorbed in the conception of European civilization, with its beginnings, on the one hand in Aryan barbarism, on the other in the Eastern and Egypto-Semitic culture, they seemed to be shut up in a certain body of conclusions about human nature and its tendencies of thought and action. What was worse, the conclusions were presented ready-made in terms of the reigning religion. But when we go to the records of the cultures and creeds of Mexico and Peru, records wonderfully preserved in the teeth of the fanaticism that would have destroyed them all if it could, we stand clear of the prejudices alike of Jew and Christian. We are spared the old contrast between pretended monotheism and polytheism, the eternal suggestion of the possible diffusion of revealed truth, the perpetual comparison between Christendom and Paganism. We are faced by a civilization and a religion that reached wealth and complexity by normal evolution from the stages of early savagery and barbarism without ever coming in contact with those of Europe till the moment of collision and destruction. And to study these American civilizations aright is to learn with clearness lessons in sociology, or human science in general, which otherwise could have been acquired only imperfectly and with hesitation. The culture-histories of the two hemispheres, put side by side, illuminate each other as do the facts of comparative anatomy.

Whatever may have been the variety of the stocks that emigrated from Asia, it holds good that we may look in the less advanced American races for traces of the steps in the religious and social evolution of Mexico and Peru. The non-Aztec peoples of Central America had developed religious systems which in their main features recall the goddess-worships of Semitic and Hellenistic antiquity; the most marked difference, as regards the historic period of the latter, being the American proclivity to human sacrifice. The summary given of some of them by H. H. Bancroft will serve to illustrate the old process by which the human mind reached the same essential results out of a superficial variety of materials:

"The most prominent personage in the Isthmian Pantheon was Dabaiba, a goddess who controlled the thunder and lightning, and with their aid devasted the lands of those who displeased her. In South America, thunder and lightning were held to be the instruments used by the sun to inflict punishment upon its enemies, which makes it probable that Dabaiba was a transformed sun-goddess. Pilgrims resorted from afar to her temple at Uraba, bringing costly presents and human victims, who were first killed and then burned, that the savory odors of roasting flesh might be grateful in the nostrils of the goddess. Some describe her as a native princess, whose reign was marked by great wisdom and many miracles, and who was apotheosized after death. She was also honored as the mother of the Creator, the maker of the sun, the moon, and all invisible things, and the sender of blessings, who seems to have acted as mediator between the people and his mother, for their prayers for rain were addressed to him, although she is described as controlling the showers, and once, when her worship was neglected, she inflicted a severe drought upon the country. When the needs of the people were very urgent, the chiefs and priests remained in the temple, fasting and praying with uplifted hands; the people meanwhile observed a four days fast, lacerating their bodies and washing their faces, which were at other times covered with paint. So strict was this fast, that no meat or drink was to be touched until the fourth day, and then only a soup made from maize flour. The priests themselves were sworn to perpetual chastity and abstinence, and those who went astray in these matters were burned or stoned to death. Their temples were encompassed with walls, and kept scrupulously clean; golden trumpets and bells with stone clappers summoned the people to worship."

NATIVE RACES OF THE PACIFIC STATES

At a lower stage of civilization we find human sacrifice already well established, on historic lines, where temples and priesthoods are still insignificant. Thus the Tupinambos of northeastern Brazil practiced a form of sacrifice which recalls at once the rite among the Indian Khonds and the better known one in Mexico, so often described. Among the lower tribes the human sacrifice figures as primarily an act either of propitiation of their own dead slain in war, or of providing them with food in the other world, they having become Gods in virtue of falling in battle and, secondarily, as an act of sacrament. The Tupinambos sought in battle not to slay but to capture enemies, and when they had a captive he was taken to their village in triumph and received with fife music, supplied by the bones of previous prisoners. For a whole year he was carefully treated, well fed and supplied with a well-favored maiden as wife and servant. At length, on the day of the feast, he was adorned with feathers, and festally led to sacrifice, his body being immediately cut in pieces and distributed among the heads of houses or minor chiefs, or, otherwise, eaten in a general feast. If he had a child by his wife, it was brought up, as among the Khonds, for the same fate.

Of the more general usage of sacrificing children, which was primordial in Central Asia, there are many traces among the North American Indians. Thus those of Florida at the time of the Spanish conquest are recorded to have sacrificed first-born children to the sun, and in Virginia there was at times offered up the sacrifice of the "only begotten son." More general seems to have been the simple usage of sacrificing boys to the God Oki and other deities. Oki was held to "suck the blood from the left breast," and the theory of the sacrifice seems to have been that it secured good fortune in war.

But there was practiced in addition an annual spring sacrifice —an instance of which is known to have occurred as late as 1837 or 1838—on the Khond principle of ensuring a good harvest, the propitiated deity in this case being the "great star" Venus. Prisoners were the usual victims, and the last and best-known case is that of the sacrifice of a Sioux maiden, who was bound to a stake and slain with arrows. Before she died pieces of her flesh were cut off in the horrible fashion of the Khonds, and the blood made to fall on the young seed corn.

Next to a human sacrifice seems to have ranked, among some tribes, that of a white dog, the dog being for the Redskin a valuable possession, and whiteness being held by them, as among the Greeks and Romans, a mark of purity and distinction in animals. Always it was something important or typically desirable that must be offered to the God. And in all cases the act of sacrifice seems to have lain near the act of sacrament, in which we know the identification of the God with the victim, whether as totem or otherwise, to have been a normal conception. The white dog, like the victim in the ancient Dionysiac sacrifice among the Greeks, seems at times to have been torn to pieces and so eaten. But there is an overwhelming amount of testimony to prove that among the Redskins at the time of the Spanish conquest religious cannabilism was common.

It was as a rule, perhaps, prisoners of war who were eaten, and it is recorded that when in the Florida war of 1528 famishing Spaniards were driven to eat the corpses of their own comrades, the Floridan natives, who were wont to eat their captives, were horror-struck—this though they had no agriculture, and fared precariously at all times. But though certain tribes were anthropophagous only on a war footing, there is only too much evidence in others that cannibalism occurred on other religious pretexts. As all primitive feasts were more or less sacramental, and the sacramental eating of human flesh is seen to have subsisted among the Aztecs long after simple cannibalism had disappeared, there can be little doubt that originally the human sacrifice was eaten among the American peoples.

Even in the "savage" stage, however, there can be traced the beginnings of the recoil not only from the sacrifice but from the cannibal sacrament. The letting of blood seems to have been in certain rites substituted for slaying, and in the story of Hiawatha the Heaven-God, who lived as a man among the Onondagas and had a mortal daughter, we find a parallel to the modified legends of Iphigeneia and Jephthah's daughter. Heaven ordered that the maiden should be sacrificed, and her father sadly brought her forth, but there came a mighty sound as of a wind, and the people, looking on high, saw a dark object approaching with terrific speed, whereupon they all fled. The father and daughter stayed resignedly, and lo! the coming thing was an enormous bird, which hurled itself with such force on the maiden that she disappeared, and the bird was buried up to the neck in the earth. Late or early, the legend was framed with a purpose.

RISE OF PRIESTHOOD

In the tribal stages, necessarily, there was little development of the priesthood. Its beginnings were represented by the "medicine men" or sorcerers, who set up secret religious societies, or orders, to at least one of which, in the historic period, sorcerers of various types and tongues could belong. Of the temple, too, the beginning is seen in the sacred hut, to which in certain tribes only the king or the medicine man has entrance, and in which begin to be stored idols and sacred objects. As we go southward, towards the region of the higher civilization, we find an increasing development of the priestly function, sometimes in combination with the kingly, as among the Natchez of Florida, among whom in the seventeenth century was found the worship of the sun, symbolized in the hut temple by an ever-burning fire. There the king-priest was "brother of the Sun," and the royal family constituted an aristocracy with special privileges, though bound to marry outside their caste.

In the midway civilizations of Central America, this development has gone far towards the state of things seen in the kingdom of the Aztecs. In Yucatan, for instance, there was a hierarchy of priests, with a head, and the order seems to have had extensive judicial powers. The temples, too, had become considerable buildings, to which the leading men made roads from their houses. Alongside of the priests, all the while, remained the sorcerers or "medicine men," also an official class with different types or orders, members of which, however, were privately employed by the nobles, after the manner of "Levites" among the early Hebrews. These private priests competed with the hierarchy in the matter of receiving formal confessions from penitents and patients. Convents existed for virgins, and of those who spent their whole lives in them the statues were after death worshipped as goddesses, while the king's daughter ranked as the "Fire Virgin," and to her others were sacrificed.

Idols of all kinds abounded, and wooden ones, like the Hebrew *teraphim*, were accounted precious family heirlooms. Human sacrifices, of course, were frequent, children being made victims in great numbers when captives were lacking, and legitimate sons when the sons of slave women ran short, not even the only son being spared. Surrogate sacrifices in the form of blood-letting were normal, but the cannibal sacrament does not seem to have been so; though it took place in Guatemala, where the king and priests and nobles partook of the victims slain to "the highest God" at the time of Lent, the high-priest and the king getting the hands and feet.

In the case of this particular sacrifice, the chosen victims, who were slaves, were each allowed for a week the peculiar privileges accorded to similar victims in the Old World, down to the detail of dining with the king; and for this sacrifice, it is recorded, the victims were "brought together in a particular house near the temple, and there got to eat and drink until they were drunk," apparently on the principles of the Khonds and Rhodians. It seems now difficult to doubt that the religion of ancient America is of Asiatic derivation, and that the pyramidal altar-temples of Mexico and Babylon are like developments from simpler mounds or "high places" shaped by the prehistoric peoples of Asia, who first carried the practice with them to the New World. It is now reasonably established that the "Mound-Builders" of the Mississippi valley were simply North American Indians, living very much at the culture stage of those found by the first whites, though there as elsewhere there may have been partial retrogression in certain tribes and territories under stress of war.

From the tribal state, civilization had risen to a stage at which, in Central America, even outside the Aztec State, as in Yucatan, there were schools in the temples where the children of the priests and nobles were taught such science as the priests possessed, from books in which had been evolved a hieratic script on the basis of hieroglyphics, as in ancient Egypt. They had advanced far in agriculture, cultivating many plants and fruits; had numerous stone buildings and excellent stone-paved roads, and had made some little progress in sculpture. But there had been no transcending of the primeval concepts of religion, and human blood flowed for the Gods far more freely than in the state of savagery. The savage's "happy hunting ground" had been specialized into a heaven and a hell; the medicine man into a great priestly order. From the primitive symbolism had been evolved the sacrament of baptism; and simple sun-worship had become a vast ceremonial. In many territories the "heathen" had so far anticipated Christian civilization as to have established the practice of confession. But the stamp of primeval savagery, conserved by the spirit of religion, is clear through it all; there is no gainsaying the fundamental relationship of the lower and the higher cults.

Around the civilizations of Peru and Mexico, at the time of the Spanish Conquest, there stretched north and south a barbarism in which we know to have existed the germs of universal historic religion—human sacrifices constituting sacraments; beliefs in deities and spirits beneficent and maleficent; practices of prayer and witchcraft, ritual and worship, festival and ordinance, the whole in part conducted by the community as a whole, but guided by the soothsayers and sorcerers who are the beginnings of priesthoods. From such antecedents everywhere has all "higher" religion been evolved.

When we turn from this stage of religious history to that of Aztec Mexico, the first and most memorable difference that faces us is the immense expansion of the power of the priests. If we can trust the Spanish writers, five thousand priests were connected with the principal temple in the city of Mexico alone, where there were in all some 600 temples, and where the total population was perhaps about 300,000, and all the cities were divided into districts placed under the charge of parochial clergy, who regulated all acts of religion. In this enormous strength of the priestly class we have the secret of that frightful development of religious delusion and its attendant atrocity which marks off Mexico from the rest of the world.

EVOLVING MYTHS

The system was polytheistic, and it exhibits the usual tendency towards pantheism or monotheism, but the overwhelming priesthood necessarily perpetuated the separate cults. There were at least thirteen principal deities, and more than two hundred inferior ones. Indeed, some reckon as high as three thousand the number of the minor spirits, who would answer to the genii and patron saints of Europe, and it is obvious that in Mexico as in Christendom there must have been many varieties of religious temper and attitude. In many of the forms of prayer and admonition which have been preserved, we see a habit of alluding reverently to "God" (*Teotl*) or "our Lord," without any specification of any one deity, and with a general assumption that the Lord loves right conduct. The universal God was in origin apparently the Sun, who was worshipped in the temples of all the Gods alike, being prayed to four times each day and four times each night.

At the first glance it is plain that the Mexican pantheon represented the myth of many tribes, myths which overlapped each other, as in the case of the ancient and widely worshipped God of Rain and his wife the Goddess of Water, and which survived separately by being adapted to the different usages of life. In connection with the rite of infant baptism, which the Mexicans practiced most scrupulously, the officiating women prayed to "Our Merciful Lady," Chalchiuhtlicue or Cioacoatl, the Goddess of Water. At the season when rain was wanted for the harvest, again, prayer was made to the God or Gods named Tlaloc—for both the singular and plural forms are used—who controlled the rain. Whereas the Goddess of Water invoked at baptism was held merciful, Tlaloc had to be propitiated by the regular sacrifice of a number of sucking infants.

There is no more awful illustration of the capacity of the human mind for religious delusion than the record of how the merciful people, believing in the efficacy of the sacrifice, would keep out of the way of the sacred procession which carried the doomed babies, because they could not bear to see them weep and think of their fate; while others, weeping themselves, would take comfort if the children wept freely, because that prognosticated plenteous rains. But even under the spell of religion men could not sacrifice infants to the very deity invoked at baptism, so the benign Water-goddess was sundered from the child-devouring Water-god. And by the same law of adaptation to social function it came about that the most prominent of the worships of Mexico, a state periodically at war, was that of the War-god Huitzilopochtli, who figured as the patron God of the nation.

In Huitzilopochtli we have a very interesting case of mythological evolution. It has been argued that he was originally a simple bird-God, his early name being the diminutive Huitziton, "the little humming bird." An old legend tells that while the Aztecs still dwelt in Aztlan, a man among them named Huitziton chirped like a bird, "Tihui"—"Let us go," and that he thus persuaded them to migrate and conquer for themselves a new country. As the later God actually bears the symbol of a humming bird on his left foot, and his name Huitzilopochtli means "humming bird on the left," there has evidently occurred some process of assimilation, but it is not quite certain that it was in this way. If the humming bird were originally a totem-God, the hypothesis would seem sound, but this, I think, has not been shown, and there remains open the possibility that the symbol was not primary but secondary.

The singular fact that, even as the Mexican War-god has a humming bird for his symbol, so Mars, the Roman War-god, has a woodpecker for his, is in this regard worth a moment's attention. We can draw no certain conclusion in the matter, but it seems likely that the evolution in the two cases may have been similar. Now there is no clear evidence that the woodpecker was a totem-God, and the whole question of Mars's name *Picumnus*, which he was held to have been from *Picus*, the woodpecker, is obscure. Oddly enough, the Sabines had a legend that the woodpecker led them to *their* settling place, which they consequently called Picenum. When we note that a number of ancient communities similarly had legends of birds or animals who guided them to their settling place, and that the name of the place sometimes accords with the name of the guide and sometimes does not, we seem obliged to recognize three possibilities:

1. The animal or bird was in some cases very likely a totem-God, the legend of guidance being a late way of explaining its association with the community.
2. A place, however, might easily be named by newcomers because

of the number of birds or animals of a given kind seen there; and the explanatory legend on that view is naught.

3. A symbolic animal, connected with the worship or image of a God, would also give rise to explanatory legends. One would prompt another.

If then the Sabines put the woodpecker on their standard, the question arises as to whether it may not have been because it was the symbol of the War-god. It is noted concerning the humming bird that he is extraordinarily brave and pugnacious, and the same might readily be said of the woodpecker, who is always attacking. Supposing the symbol to the secondary, there is no difficulty in the matter; all the legends would be intelligible on the usual lines of myth-making.

In regard to Huitzilopochtli, again, there is a symbolic source for his curious epithet "on the left." In one legend he sits after death at the left hand of his brother Tezcatlipoca, the Creator and Supreme God, and whether or not this is the earliest form of the idea, it suggests that the placing of the symbol on the left foot of the War-god may have arisen from the previous currency of the phrase "Huitzlin on the left" in another signification, though on this view the God had been already named after his symbol.

Leaving open the problem of origins, we come upon another in the fact that neither Huitzilopochtli nor Mars was primarily a War-God. The former, who was practically the national God of Mexico, was also called Mexitli, and it seems likelier that this should have been his original name, and Huitzilopochtli a sobriquet, than *vice versa*. And so with the function. A War-god, specially known as such, is not a primary conception; what happens is that a particular God comes to be the God of War. Among the Redskins, the "Great God" or Creator and Ruler, or else the Heaven or Sun-god, was the War-god, and we know that Mars was originally a sylvan deity, concerned with vegetation and flocks and herds.

How did he come to preside over war? Simply because, we may take it, he was the God of *the season at which war was usually made*. Campaigns were begun in spring, and so the God of the Spring season, who was specially invoked, became War-god. Mars was just *Martius*, March, and he lent himself the better to the conception, because March is a stormy and blusterous month. Mars strictly retains these characteristics, being a blusterous rather than a great or dignified God in both the Greek and Roman mythologies. But here suggests itself another possible source for the symbol of the War-god. *Picus* means speckled, colored, and the speckled woodpecker might figure the coming of speckled spring, as the humming bird would do the color-time in Mexico. Perhaps there may be a similar natural explanation for the further striking coincidence that Huitzilopochtli is born of a virgin mother, Coatlicue, who is abnormally impregnated by being touched by a ball of bright colored feathers, just as Juno bears Mars also virginally, being impregnated by the touch of a flower.

In both cases, certainly, we have a sufficiently marked primary type for the myth of the Virgin Birth, the idea in each being simply the birth of vegetation in spring. Though the mythical Coatlicue, like Mary, is a God-fearing woman, who frequents the temple and lives in a specified village, Coatepec, near Tula, the Virgin Mother is simply the ancient Mother of all, the Earth, and the concept of virginity is a verbally made one, in virtue of the mere fact that the whole is a metaphor. But if Huitzilopochtli be thus admittedly in origin a God of Vegetation, there arises a stronger presumption that he too was originally symbolized by his bird because of its seasonal relation to his worship. It is denied that in his case the seasonal explanation of the choice of Mars as War-god can hold good, because the spring in Mexico is a time of heavy rains, when campaigns are impossible. In his case, then, the selection of the War-god is presumably a result on the one hand of his symbol, which further seems to have been spontaneously made a symbol of the sun, and on the other hand of his special popularity—a constant feature in the cult of the Vegetation-gods.

And when we note further that the chief God of the Caribs, Yuluca, was represented with a headdress of hummingbird feathers, and that the Toltec God Quetzalcoatl, also a God of fruitfulness, was figured with the head of a sparrow, which was the hieroglyph of the air, we are led to surmise, not that all of these Gods were originally Bird-gods, but that they were all originally Spring-gods or other Nature-gods to whom the birds were given as symbols, though the sparrow *may* have been originally a totem-God. Throughout the whole of Polynesia, the red feather of one small bird, and the tail feathers of the man-of-war bird are the ordinary medium of extending or communicating supernatural power, and are regarded as specially pleasing to the Gods.

Chapter Fourteen

HUMAN SACRIFICE AND SACRAMENT

Human sacrifice, which is such a striking feature of Mexican worship, is primordial in religion, as we have seen. There can be no question that its enormous development was the work of the organized priesthood and of the cultivated religious sentiment. The Roman War-god remained subordinate, warlike though the Romans were; the Mexican became one of the two leading deities, and received the more assiduous worship. Whence the divergence? Mainly, we must conclude, from the multiplication of the Mexican priesthood, which was primarily due to the absorption of the priesthoods of the conquered races, and from the prior development of the rite of human sacrifice in the cult of the Gods or Goddesses of Vegetation.

Among the Aztecs the tradition went that human sacrifices were of late introduction, and this view would no doubt be favored by the priests, who would represent that the latter-day power of the State was due to sacrifices. But we have seen that they were practiced on a smaller scale by the American peoples at much earlier stages of social evolution, and in the midway stages they were also common. In northern South America, the chief God of the Muyscas, Fomagata, was worshipped with many human sacrifices, as he was also under the name Fomagazdad, with his wife Zipaltonal, in Nicaragua, where he and she were held to be the progenitors of the human race. Similar usages, often in connection with the Sun-god, sometimes with the God of Rain, were common in Yucatan, Chiapa, Tobasco, Honduras, and elsewhere. The Mexican Otimias, who were not conquered by the Aztecs, sacrificed children and ate their flesh, carrying it with them, roasted, on their campaigns. Such sacrifices were well established in Mexico before the Aztecs came, being found in some degree even among the relatively peaceful Toltecs. What the Aztec priesthood did was to multiply them to a frightful extent.

The causes of expansion and restriction in such cases are no doubt complex, but when we compare those of the Aztecs with the Greeks, Egyptians, and Romans, we can trace certain decisive conditions. Firstly, human sacrifices tend to multiply among peoples much given to war, by way of offerings to the Gods, but where there is only a limited priesthood the natural force of compassion leads men in time, as they grow more civilized, to abandon such sacrifices, while a priesthood tends to maintain them. Thus among the civilized peoples of the old world they lasted longest with the priest-ridden Carthaginians, and the reason that they did not continue late among the Jews was probably that these did not possess a numerous priesthood till after the Captivity, when their religion was recast in terms of the more civilized Oriental systems. On the other hand, an expanding or expanded empire, powerfully ruled by a warrior autocrat, like those of Babylon and Egypt, is led in various ways to abandon human sacrifice even if the priesthoods be numerous.

Alien cults are absorbed for political reasons, and it is no part of the ruler's policy to be habitually at war with small neighbors, having absorbed most of them; hence an irregular supply of captives. The priesthoods, too, can be conveniently provided for through other forms of sacrifice, and on those other lines they are less powerful relatively to the king. In the empire of the Incas the practice of human sacrifice was well restrained. But where a warlike and priest-ridden State is established among well-armed neighbors, with cults of human sacrifice already well-established all round, the sacrificing of captives is apt to serve as a motive to war, and the priests tend to enforce it.

The process is perfectly intelligible. The stronghold of all priesthoods is the principle of intercession, whether it be in the form of simple prayer and propitiatory worship, or a mixture of that with a doctrine of mystic sacrifice, as among Protestants, or in the constant repetition of a ceremony of mystic sacrifice, as among Catholics, or in actual animal sacrifice as among ancient Jews and pagans. In these cases we see that, the more stress is laid on the act of sacrifice, the stronger is the priesthood—or we may put it conversely. Strongest of all then must be the hold of the priesthood whose sacrifices are most terrible. And terrible was the prestige of the priesthood of Mexico.

The greater the State grew, the larger were the hecatombs of human victims. Almost every God had to be propitiated in the same way, but above all must the War-god be forever glutted with the smoking hearts of slain captives. Scarcely any historian, says Prescott, estimates the number of human beings sacrificed yearly throughout the empire at less than 20,000, and some make it 50,000. Of this doomed host, Huitzilopochtli had the lion's share, and it is recorded that at the dedication of his great new temple in 1486 there were slain in his honor 70,000 prisoners of war who had been reserved for the purpose for years throughout the empire. They formed a train two miles long, and the work of priestly butchery went on for several days.

At every festival of the God there was a new hecatomb of victims, and we may conceive how the chronic spectacle burnt itself in on the imagination of the people. The Mexican temples, as we have seen, were great pointless pyramids, sometimes of four or five stories, and the sacrifices were offered on the top. The stair was so made that it mounted successively all four sides of the pyramid, and when the train of torch-bearing priests wound their way up in the darkness, as was the rule for certain sacrifices, to the topmost platform, with its ever-burning fires and its stone of sacrifice, the whole city looked on. And then the horror of the sacrificial act!

In the great majority of the sacrifices the victim was laid living on the convex stone and held by the limbs, while the slayer cut open his breast with the sacred flint knife—the ancient knife, used before men had the use of metals, and therefore most truly religious—and tore out the palpitating heart, which was held on high to the absent but all-seeing sun, be;ore being set to burn in incense in front of the idol, whose lips, and the walls of whose shrines, were devoutly daubed with blood.

THE DEIFIED VICTIM

Apart from the resort to holocausts, the religious principle underlying many, if not all, of the American human sacrifices was that the victim *represented the God*, and on this score, slaves or children were as readily sacrificed as captives. Among the Guatemalans, we are told, captives or devoted slaves were regarded as becoming divine beings in the home of the Sun, and the general principle that the victim represented the God involved such a conception. And while this principle probably originates in early rites, such as those so long preserved by the Khonds, which aimed at the annual renewal of vegetation by propitiation and "sympathetic magic," the practice became fixed in the general rituals as a sacred thing in itself.

In connection with one annual festival of Tezcatlipoca, the Creator and "soul of the world," who combined the attributes of perpetual youthful beauty with the function of the God of justice and retribution, as Winter Sun, there was selected for immolation a young male captive of especial beauty, who was treated with great reverence for a year before being sacrificed—almost exactly like the doomed captive among the South American Tupinambos. He was gorgeously attired, flowers were strewn before him, he went about followed by a retinue of the king's pages, and the people prostrated themselves before him and worshipped him as a God. He was in fact, according to rule, the God's representative and was described as his image. A month before the fatal day, new indulgences were heaped upon him. Four beautiful maidens, bearing the names of the principal Goddesses, were given him as concubines.

At length came his death day. His honors and his joys were ended, and his fine raiment taken away. Carried on a royal barge across the lake to a particular temple, about a league from the city, whither all the people thronged, he was led up the pyramid in procession, he taking part in the ritual by throwing away his chaplets of flowers and breaking his guitar. Then, at the top, the six black-robed slayers, the sacrificial stone, and the horror of the end. And when all was over the priests piously improved the occasion, preaching that all this had been typical of human destiny, while the aristocracy sacramentally ate the victim's roasted limbs.

Along with the victim for Tezcatlipoca there was one for Huitzilopochtli, and they roamed together all the year. The latter victim was not adored, but he had the privilege of choosing the hour for his sacrifice, though not the day. He was called the "Wise Lord of Heaven," and he was slain, not on the altar, but in the arms of the priests.

The Goddesses, too, had their victims—women victims—and a maiden was regularly prepared for one sacrifice to the Maize-goddess Centeotl, the Mexican Ceres, somewhat as was the representative of Tezcatlipoca. Centeotl was the Mother-goddess *par excellence*, being named *Toucoyohua*, the "nourisher of men," and represented, like Demeter and so many Goddesses of the same type, with a child in her arms. A tradition prevailed, too, that in her cult there were anciently no human sacrifices. But this is doubtful, and the explanation is as before, that anciently single victims were sacrificed, while among the Aztecs there were many. The woman who personated the Goddess was sacrificed with other victims, and the slaying was followed by a ceremonial of an indescribably revolting character, the slayers flaying the victims and donning their skins.

This hideous act is in all likelihood one of the oldest devices of religious symbolism. Robertson Smith, in *Religion of the Semites* suggested that it is lineally connected, through the totemistic or other wearing of animal skins, with the Biblical conception of "the role of righteousness." It is certainly akin to the worship of the Fish-god, and to that of the Egyptian and other priests who wore the dappled skins of leopards or fawns as symbolizing the starry heavens, or robes without seam as symbolizing the cosmos. At bottom all ritualism is the same thing, a reduction of righteousness, in all sincerity, to make-believe.

But the special and habitual atrocity of the Mexican cultus was the act of ritual cannibalism. This was strictly a matter of religion. After a captive had been sacrificially slain in ordinary course, his body was delivered to the warrior who captured him, and was by him made the special dish at a formal and decorous public banquet to his friends. It was part of the prescribed worship of the Gods. That the Mexicans were not in the least cannibals by taste is shown by the fact that in the great siege of Cortes they died of starvation by thousands. They never ate fellow citizens; only the sacrificially slain captive.

But only a great priesthood could have maintained even that usage. We have seen that such ritual cannibalism has existed at one time in all races, and obviously it must have originated in simple cannibalism, for men would never have begun to offer to the Gods food that was primordially abominable to themselves. On the other hand, however, we know that cannibalism everywhere dies out naturally even among savages, apart from religion, as soon as they reach some degree of peaceful life, and even sooner. Among the native tribes of Lower California, though they were among the most degraded savages in the world, and given to various disgusting practices, the eating not only of human flesh but of that of monkeys, as resembling men, is held abominable. The Tahitians, who in warfare were murderous to the last degree, and practiced hideous barbarities, had evolved beyond the stage of public cannibal banquests. Even the sacrifice of a man to the God was followed only by the pretended eating of his eye by the chief, and it was the priests who instigated what human sacrifices there were. So among the similarly curel Tongans, cannibal feasts were rare, occurring only after battles, and being execrated by the women. Child sacrifices were also rare and special, and were superseded by surrogates of amputated fingers.

In each of these cases the priesthoods were little organized; hence the upward evolution. Among the Fijians, the Marquesans, and the Maoris, on the contrary, we find highly organized and cannibalistic priesthoods, and there we find cannibalism and human sacrifices are common. So, among the Khonds, a specially "instructed" priest was essential to the *meriah* sacrifices, and in China, where human scapegoat sacrifices were discredited and abolished between the third and second centuries B.C., we hear of them being prescribed by priests and put down by wise rulers. And as in Peru the Incas put some check on human sacrifice, so in the whole of Central America the only case of any attempt at such reform, apart from the Toltec priesthood of Quetzalcoatl, occurs in the history of the great Acolhuan king of Tezcuco, Netzahualcoyotl, who died in 1472. Of him it is told that he was the best poet of his country, which was the most highly civilized of the New World, and that he worshipped on a great altar-pyramid of nine stages an "unknown God," who had no image, and to whom he offered only perfume and incense, resisting the priests who pressed for human sacrifice. But his example seems never to have affected his Aztec allies, who gradually won supremacy over the Tezcucans, and even in his own realm he could never suppress the human sacrifices which had there been revived before his time under Aztec influence, and multiplied under it later.

The Aztec religion, in fine, was working the ruin of the civilization of Central America, as similar religions may have done for the far older civilizations that have left only ruins behind them. Sacerdotalism, it is clear, tended as an institution to check the progress of humanity, which even among slaughterous savages elsewhere brought anthropophagy into discredit. No amount of passion for war could have kept the civilized Aztecs complacently practicing ritual cannibalism if an austere and all-powerful priesthood had not fanatically enforced it. The great sanction for human sacrifice, with the Mexicans as with the Semites, was the doctrine which identified the God with the victim, and as it were sacrificed him to himself. The principle was thus in a peculiar degree priest-made and priest-preserved.

MEXICAN ETHNICS

The recital of these facts may lead some to conclude that the Mexican priesthood must have been the most atrocious multitude of miscreants the world ever saw. But that would be a complete misconception; they were as conscientious a priesthood as history bears record of. The strangest thing of all is that their frightful system of sacrifice was bound up not only with a strict and ascetic sexual morality, but with an emphatic humanitarian doctrine.

If asceticism be virtue, they cultivated virtue zealously. There was a Mexican Goddess of Love, and there was of course plenty of vice, but nowhere could men win a higher reputation for sanctity by living in celibacy. Their saints were numerous. They had nearly all the formulas of Christian morality, so-called. The priests themselves mostly lived in strict celibacy, and they educated children with the greatest vigilance in their temple schools and higher colleges. They taught the people to be peaceful; to bear injuries with meekness; to rely on God's mercy and not on their own merits. They taught, like Jesus and the pagans, that adultery could be committed by the eyes and the heart, and above all they exhorted men to feed the poor.

The public hospitals were carefully attended, at a time when some Christian countries had none. They had the practice of confession and absolution, and in the regular exhortation of the confessor there was this formula: "Clothe the naked and feed the hungry, whatever privations it may cost thee; cherish the sick, for they are the image of God." And in that very same exhortation there was further urged on the penitent the special duty of procuring instantly *a slave for sacrifice to the deity.*

Such phenomena carry far the challenge to conventional sociology. These men, judged by religious standards, closely compare with our European typical priesthood. They doubtless had the same temperamental qualities; a strong irrational sense of duty; an hysterical habit of mind, a certain spirit of self-sacrifice, at times a passion for asceticism, and a feeling that sensuous indulgence was revolting. Devoid of moral *science*, they had plenty of the blind instinct to do right. They devoutly did what their religion told them, even as Catholic priests have devoutly served the Inquisition. That is one of the central sociological lessons of our subject. The religious element in man, being predominantly emotional and traditional, may ally itself with either good or evil, and no thanks are due to religion, properly speaking, if it is ever in any degree identified with good.

How is it that Christianity is not associated with human sacrifice while the Mexican cultus was? Simply by reason of the different civilizations that went before. It is civilization that determines the tone of religion and not the other way. Christianity starts with a doctrine of one act of human sacrifice, and Christians are specially invited each year at the sacred season to fasten their minds on the details of that act. Their ritual keeps up the mystic pretence of the act of ritual cannibalism which of old went with the human sacrifice; they harp on the very words, "body and blood." They mystically eat the body of the slain God. Now this very act was performed by the Mexicans not only literally, as we have seen, but in the symbolic way also, and they connected their sacraments with the symbol of the cross.

THE GOD ON THE CROSS

Of the Tlascalans it is told that at one festival they fixed a prisoner to a high cross and shot arrows at him, and that at another time they fastened one to a low cross and killed him by bastinado. In the sacrifice of a maiden to the Maice-goddess Centeotl, the priest who wore the slain victim's skin stood with his arms outstreched, crosswise, before the image of Huitzilopochtli, so representing the Goddess, and the skin (presumably stuffed) was hung up with the arms spread in the same attitude, and facing the street. The Mexicans, finally, had a festival in honor of Xiuhteuctli, the God of Fire, the crowning act of which was the making of a dough image of the God (as was done in the worship of Huitzilopochtli, at the festival called "Eating the God") and *raising it on a cross*, the image being then eaten by the crowd as possessing a sacred efficacy. They felt they were brought into union with the God in that fashion.

There is some evidence that among the first Christians the eucharist was sometimes a baked dough image of a child, and on any view the irresistible presumption is that in all cases alike the symbolical usage grew out of a more ancient practice of ritual cannibalism. Christianity coming among a set of civilized peoples, the symbol became more and more mystical, though the priesthood adhered tenaciously to the doctrine of daily mystical sacrifice. In Mexico, certain cults had similarly substituted symbolism for actual sacrifice; among the modifying practices being the drawing of a little blood from the ears and other parts of the children of the aristocracy. But the thin end of the wedge was in, so to speak, in the survival of actual human sacrifices, and the Aztec priesthood drove the wedge deeper and deeper, in virtue of their collective economic interest as well as of what we may term the master tendency of all religions —the fixation of ideas and usages. The more piety the more priests; the more priests the more sacrifices; and the constant wars of the Aztecs supplied an unfailing stream of captives for immolation.

Many wars were made for the sole purpose of obtaining captives; in fact, the Aztec kings made a treaty with the neighboring republic of Tlascala and its confederates, a treaty which was faithfully kept, to the effect that their armies should fight on a given ground at stated seasons, in order that *both* sides should be able to supply themselves with sacrificial victims. At all other times they were quite friendly, and the Aztec kings avowedly kept up the relation purely in order to have captives for sacrifice. An arrangement like that, once set up, would flourish more and more up to the point of national exhaustion, especially as death in battle was reckoned a sure passport to Paradise. The priesthood would at the same time grow ever more and more numerous, the only limit being the people's power of endurance. There can be little doubt that the Aztec empire would ultimately have broken down under its monstrous burden if the Spaniards had not destroyed it; for the taxation necessary to support the military and aristocratic system alongside of the allocation of enormous untaxed domains to the ever-multiplying myriads of priests was becoming more insupportable year by year, so that the deep disaffection of the common people was one of the chief supports to the campaign of Cortes. It may well be that some of the previous civilizations had succumbed in the same way, literally destroyed by religion to the extent of inviting conquest by less "civilized" tribes. Among some of the Maya peoples, who preceded the Aztecs, the office of sacrificer had come to be regarded as degraded, but even there the sacrifices never ceased, and the Maya civilization failed to hold its ground before the others.

Strangely enough, there was current among the Aztecs themselves a belief that their State was doomed to be overthrown. Here, doubtless, we have a clue to the existence of civilizing forces, and of a spirit of hostility to the religion of bloodshed which, however, felt driven to express itself in terms of despair. To this spirit of betterment, then, we turn with the doubled interest of sympathy.

THE MEXICAN WHITE CHRIST

Two sets of phenomena tell of the presence among the Aztecs of that instinct of humanity or spirit of reason which elsewhere gradually delivered men from the demoralization of human sacrifice. One was the practice, already noted, of substituting a symbol for the sacrificed victim; the other was the cultus of the relatively benign deity Quetzalcoatl, a God of the Toltecs whom the Aztecs had subdued. There is no more striking figure in American mythology.

The name appears to have meant "the feathered (or colored) serpent," and this was one of his symbols, but he was normally represented by the red-billed sparrow-head, which in Mexican hieroglyphics stands for the air. His third symbol, the Firestone, had the same significance. As God of the Air, accordingly, he ranks in the pantheon. But his mythus had a uniquely ethical stamp, and a certain wistful pathos. It tells that he was once high priest at Tula, in Anahuac, where, ever clothed in white, he founded a cultus, and gave beneficent laws to men, teaching them also the arts of agriculture, metal-work, stone-cutting, and civil government; the while a king named Huemac held with him the secular rule, and framed the law book of the nation. But the God Tezcatlipoca came to earth in the guise of a young merchant, who deceived the king's daughter; and in the guise of an old man, who persuaded Quetzalcoatl to drink a mystic drink, whereupon he was seized with an irresistible impulse to wander away. And so he went south-eastwards, setting up his institutions in place after place, but always going farther, till at length he disappeared in the east, with a promise to return. For that return his worshippers looked ever longingly, and the Aztec kings looked with fear, till when Cortes came all thought that he was the God, and at Cholula the people sacrificed a man to him, and daubed him with the blood in the regulation way.

But in the myth of Quetzalcoatl it is told that at Tula he had preached against human sacrifices, telling men to offer to the Gods only fruits and flowers, and that he could not endure the thought of war, closing his ears when men spoke of it. A similar doctrine is associated with the traditional worship of the rival God Wotan, the legendary founder of the Maya civilization, and it may be that in both cases there is a reversion to the memory of simpler and kindlier cults. In any case, this humane legend figures for us a late product of Toltec feeling, representing at once the aspiration for a better religion and the memory of the Toltec people, whose polity had been step by step driven to the southeast by the stronger power of the Aztecs.

It may have been some of the Toltec priests who remained under Aztec rule who framed the gentle mythus, and so dreamed for themselves a Messiah, as so many conquered races had done before. On analysis, it appears that Huemac was really the old Toltec name of the God, and that he took that of Quetzalcoatl in one of his more southerly resting places, when he became symbolized as the serpent. Of old he had had human sacrifices like other Gods, and in the Aztec lands he had them still. But some of his white-robed priests, left victimless till they recoiled from the bloody rites of their conquerors, felt that their God must have a different nature from that of the Gods of the blackrobed priests of Tezcatlipoca and Huitzilopochtli, and so framed for his cult a new gospel.

Recognizing this, Muller and Brinton and Reville agree that Quetzalcoatl is properly the God of the beneficent rain-bringing east wind, identified with the vanished Toltec people, so that like them he is driven away by the enmity of other deities, but, like the vanishing or slain Sun-god of all mythologies, he is to return again in power and great glory. By such a myth Christians are set vaguely surmising a debt to their own legend, but there is no such thing in this case. As Bancroft observes, following Muller, the process is one which has occurred in many mythologies:

"It is everywhere the case among savages, with their national God, that the latter is a nature-deity, who becomes gradually transformed into a national God, then into a national King, high priest, founder of a religion, and at last ends in being considered a human being. The older and purer the civilization of a people is, the easier it is to recognize the original essence of its national God, in spite of all transformations and disguises. So it is here. Behind the human form of the God glimmers the nature-shape, and the national God is known by, perhaps, all his worshippers as a nature-deity. From his powerful influence upon nature, he might also be held as creator. The pure human form of this God (Quetzalcoatl) as it appears in the fable, as well as in the image, is not the original but the youngest. His oldest concrete forms are taken from nature, to which he originally belongs, and have maintained themselves in many attributes. All these symbolize him as the God of fertility, chiefly . . . by means of the beneficial influence of the air."

What is specially interesting is that, despite the inner hostility of the Quetzalcoatl cult to those of the Mexican gods, his stood in high honor, and while some of his devotees sacrificed and ate his representative once a year in the usual manner, some of his priests, of whom the chief also bore his name as representing him, did as little sacrificing as they could, evidently finding some support in that course. We are moved to ask, then, whether there was here a culture force that could have countervailed the host of the priests of slaughter had the Aztecs been left to work out their own salvation. The more the problem is pondered, however, the less probable will it seem that the humaner teaching could have so triumphed. Conquest by some other American people might have served to restrain the religion of blood, but there is no sign that the humaner cult was as such making serious headway.

The Aztec priesthood like every other had an economic basis; its higher offices were the perquisites of certain aristocratic families, and the habit of perpetual bloodshed had atrophied the feelings of the priestly army on that side. Beyond a certain point, priesthoods are incapable of intellectual regeneration from within, even if reformative ideas be present.

THE FATALITY OF THE PRIESTHOOD

The main hope of the humaner thinkers would probably lie in the substitution of a symbolic for an anthropophagous sacrament; if baked effigies could be eaten, effigies might be sacrificed.

But in some even of the symbolic sacraments blood was a constituent. Thus in the cult of Huitzilopochtli, for the baked image made of seeds for the winter festival of the solstice—Christmas—the blood of slain children was the cementing moisture. Here again we have the primitive "sympathetic magic," the image, which was transfixed with an arrow before being eaten, represented the potentialities of new vegetable life at the time of year when vegetation was dead. The blood of children was the deadly symbol of the moisture that was the life of all things, besides being a means of, as it were, vitalizing the image. Such a cult was indeed far from reducing anthropophagy to a mere symbol.

So with the cult of Xiuhteuctle, the Fire-god. Alongside, apparently, of the remarkable symbolic sacrament above mentioned there were anthropophagous sacraments to the same God. He was one of the most widely honored of all, the first drink at every meal in every household being taken in his name—a correlation which again suggests derivation from an Asiatic fire cult such as is seen blended in that of Agni in the Vedas. In his name, too, every child was passed through the fire at birth—another notable parallel to ancient Asiatic usages—and from his six hundred temples burned as many perpetual fires. Every four years a great feast was held in his honor at Quauhtitlan, not far from the city of Mexico, the first act being to plant six high trees before the temple on the day previous, and to sacrifice two slaves, who were flayed. On the feast day, two priests appeared clad in those victims' skins, hailed with the cry, "See, there come our Gods," and all day they danced to wild music, while many thousands of quails were sacrificed to the God. Finally the priests took six prisoners and bound or hanged them to the tops of the six trees, where they were shot through with arrows. When dead they were taken down and their hearts cut out in the usual way, the priests and nobility finally eating the flesh of both the men and the quails as a sacrament.

It is not clear at what place and period the symbolical sacrifice in this cult arose, but the essential problem is whether it could have ousted the other. And the answer must be that inasmuch as the human sacrifice was specially associated with the power of the priests, and was obviously to the tastes of the mass of the people of all grades, nothing short of an overthrow of the existing polity by another could have effected the transformation, there being no native culture in the surrounding States that could give the requisite moral lead on a large scale. Such violent subversion, it will be remembered, was a common condition of religious evolution in the Old World in antiquity, and the history of the great priestly systems of Egypt, India, and Babylon points to the conclusion that not otherwise than by the fiat of powerful autocrats, or forcible overthrow at the hands of neighboring and kindred races, in the absence of peaceful culture contacts of a higher kind, could such systems be made to loosen their grasp on social and intellectual life.

It will be observed that in the cult under notice the priest represents the God even as does the victim. The same phenomenon occurs, sometimes, though not always, with the same procedure of donning the victim's skin, in many of the American sacrificial cults, Aztec and other. A recent hierologist has argued, in view of the various instances in which priest-kings and sacrificial priests have been themselves annually sacrificed, that it was as the shedder of divine (victim's) blood that the king-priest's blood was shed, and that he was originally distinguished from his fellow-worshippers only by his greater readiness to sacrifice himself for their religious needs. We need not dwell here on the fallacy of thus imputing a calculated and reasoned self-devotion in the case of an act which, among savage men, would stand just as much for lack of imagination or forethought. Assuming the theory to be true, however, we must recognize that in the case of the historic Mexican priesthood any ancient liability of the kind had long disappeared. According to Herrera, the private chaplains of the nobles were slain at the death of their masters, but this was as slaves or attendants, not as public priests, and not as true sacrifices. In not a single case do we learn that the victim was furnished by the priestly class. That class indeed practiced, in some measure, as we have seen, the asceticisms common to most ancient priesthoods, but it had long made an end of any serious penalties attaching to its profession. The priests, in short, were the dominant force in the Mexican society, and under them it was, on the one hand, being economically ruined in the manner of most ancient empires, and on the other, being anchylosed in its moral and intellectual life. To say this is of course not to select the priests for blame as being the sole or primary causes of the fatal development; their order was but the organized expression of the general religious tendency. But they dramatically exhibit, once for all, the capacity of "religion" in general to darken life and blight civilization.

The mere number of the priests was so great as to constitute a force of fixation such as has never been countervailed in modern European countries, where forces relatively less powerful have only slowly been undermined by culture influences from more advanced neighboring communities. When we note that the temple of the Mexican Wine-god alone had four hundred priests, we realize that we are in the presence of social conditions which mere humanism could not avail to transform, even if it found a hearing among the priesthoods. A fortiori, no philosophic developments on the sacerdotal side could have availed. The growth of a pantheistic philosophy among the priesthoods of ancient India, Babylonia and Egypt, and the growth of a monotheistic doctrine among those of Jewry, were equally without effect on the sacerdotal practices as a whole, these remaining in all cases alike primitively sacrificial, though, for extra-sacerdotal reasons already noted, they ceased to include human sacrifice. And in Mexico, of course, the philosophic developments were slight at best. The figuring of Tezcatlipoca as "the soul of the world" does not appear to have stood for any methodically pantheistic thought, being apparently an expression of henotheism common in solar worships. The entire Mexican civilization, in short, was being arrested at a stage below that attained in the Mesopotamian empires long before the Christian era.